101 Great Lowfat Desserts

How to Order:

Single copies may be ordered from Prima Publishing, P.O. Box 1260BK, Rocklin, CA 95677; telephone (916) 632-4400. Quantity discounts are also available. On your letterhead, include information concerning the intended use of the books and the number of books you wish to purchase.

101
Great Lowfat Desserts

No Butter, No Cream, No Kidding!

Donna Rodnitzky

PRIMA PUBLISHING

Production by Melanie Field, Strawberry Field Publishing
Copyediting by Jane Gilligan
Illustrations by Martha Gilman Roach
Typography by Archetype Book Composition
Interior design by Suzanne Montazer, SLM Graphics
Cover design by The Dunlavey Studio, Sacramento

Library of Congress Cataloging-in-Publication Data

Rodnitzky, Donna.
   101 great lowfat desserts: no butter, no cream, no kidding!
Donna Ronitzky.
     p. cm.
   Includes index.
   ISBN 1-55958-666-4
   1. Desserts. 2. Low-fat diet—Recipes. I. Title. II. Title:
One hundred one great lowfat desserts.
TX773.R63 1995
641.8′6—dc20   94-33548
                                        CIP

95 96 97 98 99 RRD 10 9 8 7 6 5 4 3 2 1
Printed in the United States of America

To my husband, Bob, and my children,
David, Adam, and Laura, who offered their
enthusiastic support and encouragement

Contents

Cookies and Bars   65

Muffins   123

Layer Cakes, Cheesecakes, Puddings, and Other Desserts 166

Special Occasion Cakes 230

Cake Decorations   273

°Courtesy of the California Prune Board

Acknowledgments

A very special thank you to Terri Nelson, RD/LD, who provided the nutritional analysis of all the recipes in the cookbook.

I also wish to thank Patricia Redlinger, Ph.D., who helped me to understand the properties of gluten.

Introduction

Imagine yourself enjoying a slice of sinfully rich, moist chocolate torte, covered with a heavenly chocolate glaze and topped with a white chocolate rose. Now imagine you are told that this exquisite dessert contains no butter or shortening but instead was made with puréed fruit, allowing its fat content to be reduced by 75 to 90 percent and its calories by 20 to 30 percent. Well, you no longer have to fantasize about indulging in such desserts. This revolutionary reduced-fat dessert cookbook contains outstanding recipes for elegant tortes, rich layer cakes, irresistable cookies, and sweet breads, all made without butter or fat but having the same taste, texture, and appearance found in fat-laden desserts. Many of these desserts are simple pleasures while others can be attractively adorned to transform them into culinary masterpieces you would be proud to serve to your most distinguished guests.

I have revealed the secret to creating these delicious reduced-fat desserts and I must acknowledge the California Prune Board for entrusting me with it. I wrote this lowfat dessert cookbook based on an exciting new method of baking they discovered. Marketing surveys have found that the fat content of food is a primary nutritional and health concern of many Americans. On the other hand, the surveys reveal that these same members of the fat posse retain their desire to splurge on rich desserts. With this apparent paradox of self-indulgence and self-control in mind, the Prune Board realized the potential of using its favorite fruit as a fat substitute in baking. Food technologists then developed recipes in which puréed prunes were substituted for butter and fat on a one-for-one basis with no detectable loss of moisture and texture. This is because prunes and many other fruits are high in pectin and naturally occuring sorbitol (a mildly sweet sugar alcohol), which act as humectants that attract and bind moisture. When butter or shortening is used in baked goods, the foods stay moist because the fat creates a film around the gluten in the flour and prevents water from escaping. The humectant quality in prune purée not only keeps baked goods moist, it also provides the "mouthfeel" usually associated with fat-laden desserts. These two qualities are also long lasting, so that desserts made with fruit purées stay fresh for a very long time. In fact, you may find yourself wishing they would grow stale so you could have an excuse to bake more.

As I have learned, not only prunes but almost any kind of puréed fruit can be used in place of fat or shortening in baking. The same one-for-one replacement applies and results in desserts that are equally delicious.

Much to my dismay, however, when I first started testing fruit-substituted recipes, I seemed to have more failures than successes. My desserts had a rubbery texture and were very unappetizing. After doing some additional research, I discovered the problem. In food preparation, gluten is formed when flour is moistened and stirred. Gluten acts as the structural framework, with fat and sugar the tenderizing agents, and these two effects must always be balanced. When shortening is added to the batter or dough, it acts as a lubricant. This makes the dough tender by coating gluten strands so that they slide past rather than cling to each other. This also gives the finished product richness and tenderness. Fruit purées also have this quality. Yet they cause additional hydration of the gluten strands. Consequently, when the batter is beaten vigorously, the gluten becomes overdeveloped and the resulting product has a tough texture instead of a tender crumb. This can be avoided by gently mixing the recipes by hand rather than with a mixer. In the first step, the dry ingredients are combined in a large mixing bowl and the wet ingredients are combined in a smaller bowl. In the second step, the wet mixture is added to the dry mixture. I like to tilt the bowl slightly and rotate it as I combine the ingredients with a fork until just blended. (This procedure is very similar to the way muffins are properly prepared.) One other helpful note: To preserve moisture in the baked goods, I call for waxed paper to cover the breads and cakes while cooling—a technique first taught to me by my mother.

Although any kind of puréed fruit can be used in place of fat or shortening, in chocolate desserts I prefer using prune lekvar, a prune butter available in most supermarkets. The combination of prune lekvar and chocolate produces chocolate cakes that are exceptionally moist and rich, and the chocolate flavor is not at all affected by the taste of the prunes. In fact, whenever I have served one of my signature chocolate tortes to guests, they have been amazed to learn that a cake so delicious was made with prunes and not butter. In recipes where I am more concerned about color, I prefer to use pear baby food. Of course, the variety of fruit used is a matter of taste, and most can be used interchangeably in these recipes. Substitute any of the puréed dried fruits, applesauce, or a fruit of your choice.

All of the recipes in this cookbook have been analyzed for their fat and caloric content. The American Heart Association recommends that in our daily diet the percentage of calories derived from fat should not exceed 30 percent. As important as it is to reduce fat, for most of us the number of calories consumed daily should also be kept to a certain amount. Most of the recipes in this book will help you meet both of these healthful dietary standards. One important fact must be kept in mind: Although this book provides recipes that are *lower* in fat, it is important to realize that they are not fat-*free*. The thrust of the book is *reduction* in fat by substituting fruit for butter or shortening. An occasional recipe is slightly higher in calories and the percentage of fat but even these—included for those very special occasions—have less calories and fat than comparable items baked the ordinary way.

I am always looking for new recipes and ideas so that I can add variety as well as taste to meal planning. Like many health-conscious people, I restrict the percentage of fat in the foods I prepare for my family and friends. At the same time, I have a passion for gourmet cuisine and fancy desserts. That I could develop some of the elegant reduced-fat desserts in this book was therefore especially rewarding for me. Many of the recipes included are adaptions of those I learned from my mother, who was a constant source of culinary inspiration while I was growing up. Additional recipes came from friends, my own collection of recipes, and frequently from people who heard about my efforts and asked me to *please* reduce the fat in one of their favorite recipes. Once I understood the chemistry of this new kind of baking, I thoroughly enjoyed the venture. I hope you derive as much pleasure from creating and indulging in these reduced-fat desserts and that it will convince you, as it has me, that health-conscious dining doesn't have to be boring.

About the Nutritional Information

Nutritional information is provided for each recipe in this book. It is important to note that the nutritional analysis may vary slightly depending on the brands of food that are used. If a recipe contains a "trace" of a particular item (less than 1/2 gram of protein, total fat, saturated fat, or carbohydrate or less than 1/2 milligram of sodium or cholesterol), the number will be listed as zero.

Note: Serving sizes are generally smaller.

Helpful Hints

Many of the recipes in this cookbook suggest using prune lekvar as a fat substitute in baking. Although lekvar (a sweet purée of cooked plums or prunes) is easy to make, I prefer to use premade *Solo* Prune Plum (Lekvar) Filling, which comes in a 12-ounce can. It is found in the dried fruit, pie fillings, or baking section in most supermarkets.

If you want to make your own fruit butter or purée, experiment with any of your favorite dried fruits. Here are the recipes for the fruit butters I use most often when I bake:

Prune Butter: Combine 1 1/3 cups of pitted chopped prunes with 6 tablespoons of water in the work bowl of a food processor; process until the prunes are puréed. Makes 1 cup.

Date Butter: Combine 1 cup of chopped dates with 6 tablespoons of water in the work bowl of a food processor; process until the dates are puréed. Makes 3/4 cup.

Apricot Butter: Combine 1 cup of dried chopped apricots with 6 tablespoons of water in the work bowl of a food processor; process until apricots are puréed. Makes 3/4 cup.

There are many reduced-fat or nonfat products available now for use in baking. I have tried to include many of them in my cookbook, while at the same time aiming to make the desserts as rich-tasting as possible. However, depending on your individual tastes and health requirements, you may wish to experiment by using more or less of these ingredients to fashion a dessert that is tailor-made for you.

Sweet Breads and Coffee Cakes

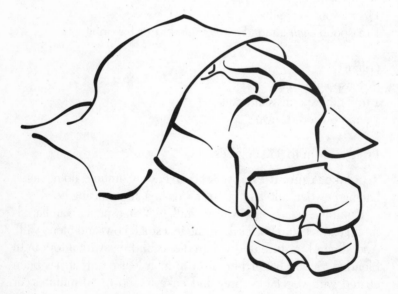

Almond Poppy Seed Bread

The slightly nutty flavor of the poppy seeds and the rich almond flavoring produce a deliciously sweet bread. Serve it with fresh berries or offer it as a housewarming gift.

12 servings

Almond Poppy Seed Bread
1 3/4 cups unbleached flour
1 1/4 cups granulated sugar
1 1/2 teaspoons baking powder
1/4 teaspoon salt
2 tablespoons poppy seeds
1 jar (6 ounces) pear baby food
2 egg whites
3/4 cup skim milk
1 1/2 teaspoons vanilla
1 teaspoon *each* almond extract and butter flavoring

Glaze
1/2 teaspoon vanilla
1 to 2 tablespoons skim milk
1 cup powdered sugar

Preheat oven to 350 degrees.

To make Almond Poppy Seed Bread: Combine flour, sugar, baking powder, salt, and poppy seeds in a large mixing bowl.

Combine pears, egg whites, milk, 1 1/2 teaspoons vanilla, almond extract, and butter flavoring in a small bowl and blend well. Add almond mixture to dry ingredients and mix with a fork until blended. Spoon batter into a 9 × 5-inch loaf pan that has been coated with vegetable spray and bake for 55 to 60 minutes, or until cake tester inserted into center of bread comes out clean.

Cover bread with waxed paper and cool on a cake rack. When bread is cool, remove from pan.

To make glaze: Gradually add 1/2 teaspoon vanilla and enough milk to powdered sugar to make a glaze thick enough to spoon over bread; do not make it runny. Spoon glaze over cooled bread, allowing it to run down the sides. Let glaze harden before storing the bread in an airtight container. The bread tastes best when allowed to sit for 24 hours.

Nutritional analysis per serving:

Bread:

168	Calories	6 %	Calories from Fat
4 g	Protein	2 g	Fiber
37 g	Carbohydrates	105 mg	Sodium
1 g	Fat	0 mg	Cholesterol

Glaze:

35	Calories	0 %	Calories from Fat
0 g	Protein	0 g	Fiber
8 g	Carbohydrates	1 mg	Sodium
0 g	Fat	0 mg	Cholesterol

Total:

203	Calories	5 %	Calories from Fat
4 g	Protein	2 g	Fiber
45 g	Carbohydrates	106 mg	Sodium
1 g	Fat	0 mg	Cholesterol

Apple Spice Cake

I found this recipe in a Dannon Yogurt advertisement in the newspaper. The cake is nicely spiced, very moist, and easy to prepare.

24 servings

2 3/4 cups unbleached flour
2 1/4 cups sugar
2 1/2 teaspoons baking soda
1 1/4 teaspoons baking powder
1 teaspoon cinnamon
1/2 teaspoon *each* allspice and salt
1/4 teaspoon ground cloves
1 cup raisins
1 cup applesauce
1 1/4 cups plain nonfat yogurt
1/3 cup prune lekvar
3 egg whites

Preheat oven to 325 degrees.

Combine flour, sugar, baking soda, baking powder, cinnamon, allspice, salt, cloves, and raisins in a large mixing bowl.

Combine applesauce, yogurt, lekvar, and egg whites in a medium-size mixing bowl; blend until smooth. Add applesauce mixture to dry ingredients and mix with a fork until blended. Spoon batter into a greased and floured 10-inch Bundt pan and bake for 60 to 65 minutes, or until cake tester inserted into center of cake comes out clean. Cover cake with waxed paper and cool on a cake rack for 25 minutes. Remove cake from pan, recover with waxed paper, and let cool completely. Store in an airtight container.

Nutritional analysis per serving:

160	Calories	1 %	Calories from Fat
3 g	Protein	1 g	Fiber
38 g	Carbohydrates	164 mg	Sodium
0 g	Fat	0 mg	Cholesterol

3 points

Apricot Coffee Cake

My mother was renowned for her fabulous cooking. She loved to collect recipes and would try to make them at least once. While looking through her recipe box, I found a recipe for Apricot Coffee Cake. It called for butter, eggs, milk, and cream cheese which produced a deliciously rich cake. This reduced-fat version is not as rich, but still delicious.

21 servings

Topping
1/4 cup flour
3 tablespoons granulated sugar
1 1/2 tablespoons light margarine
1 teaspoon cinnamon

Cake
2 cups unbleached flour
1 cup sugar
1 teaspoon baking powder
1/2 teaspoon baking soda
1/8 teaspoon salt
1 package (8 ounces) light cream cheese, at room temperature
1 jar (6 ounces) pear baby food
1/2 cup skim milk
1/2 cup egg substitute
1 1/2 teaspoons vanilla
2/3 cup good-quality apricot preserves
Powdered sugar to dust cake (optional)

Preheat oven to 350 degrees.

To make topping: Using a fork, combine flour, sugar, margarine, and cinnamon until crumbly. Spoon topping into the bottom of a 9-inch Bundt pan that has been coated with vegetable spray. Set pan aside.

To make cake: Combine flour, sugar, baking powder, baking soda, and salt in a large mixing bowl.

In work bowl of food processor, process cream cheese until smooth. Add pears, milk, egg substitute, and vanilla and process until blended. Add cream cheese mixture to dry ingredients and mix with a fork until blended. Spoon half of batter into prepared Bundt pan. Spread apricot preserves onto batter leaving a 1-inch border to both inner and outer edge of pan. Top with remaining batter and bake for 50 to 55 minutes, or until cake tester inserted into center of cake comes out clean. Cover cake with waxed paper and cool on a cake rack. When cake is cool, remove from pan and store in an airtight container. Dust top of cake with powdered sugar before serving, if desired.

Nutritional analysis per serving:

Topping:

12	Calories	0 %	Calories from Fat
0 g	Protein	0 g	Fiber
3 g	Carbohydrates	4 mg	Sodium
0 g	Fat	0 mg	Cholesterol

Cake:

143	Calories	17 %	Calories from Fat
3 g	Protein	1 g	Fiber
26 g	Carbohydrates	101 mg	Sodium
3 g	Fat	8 mg	Cholesterol

Total:

155	Calories	17 %	Calories from Fat
3 g	Protein	1 g	Fiber
29 g	Carbohydrates	105 mg	Sodium
3 g	Fat	8 mg	Cholesterol

---

3 points

Banana Bread

Bananas are high in vitamins A, B$_2$, and C. All that goodness can be enjoyed in this delicious, moist bread.

10 servings

1 1/2 cups unbleached flour
3/4 cup sugar
1 teaspoon baking soda
1/8 teaspoon salt
3 ripe bananas
2 egg whites
1 jar (6 ounces) applesauce baby food

Preheat oven to 350 degrees.

Combine flour, sugar, baking soda, and salt in a large mixing bowl.
　　Place bananas in work bowl of food processor and purée. Add egg whites and applesauce and process until smooth. Add banana mixture to dry ingredients and mix with a fork until blended. Spoon batter into a 9 × 5-inch loaf pan that has been coated with vegetable spray and bake for 45 to 50 minutes, or until cake tester inserted into center of bread comes out clean. Cover bread with waxed paper and cool on a cake rack. Store in an airtight container.

Nutritional analysis per serving:

161	Calories	3 %	Calories from Fat
4 g	Protein	3 g	Fiber
38 g	Carbohydrates	120 mg	Sodium
1 g	Fat	0 mg	Cholesterol

Banana-Chocolate Cake

The combination of chocolate and bananas in this very moist cake tastes almost as good as a frozen chocolate-covered banana!

21 servings

1/3 cup chocolate chips
2 tablespoons water
2 cups unbleached flour
1 cup sugar
3/4 teaspoon baking soda
1/2 teaspoon baking powder
1/8 teaspoon salt
2 ripe bananas
1 jar (6 ounces) pear baby food
1/2 cup nonfat sour cream
1/2 cup egg substitute
1 1/2 teaspoons vanilla

Preheat oven to 350 degrees.

Melt chocolate chips and water in a small heavy saucepan, covered, over low heat. When chocolate is soft, blend well. Set aside.

Combine flour, sugar, baking soda, baking powder, and salt in a large mixing bowl.

In work bowl of food processor, purée bananas. Add pears, sour cream, egg substitute, and vanilla and blend well. Add banana mixture to dry ingredients and mix with a fork until blended. Spoon one-third of the batter into a 9-inch Bundt pan that has been coated with vegetable spray. Spoon one-half of the melted chocolate onto batter leaving a 1/2-inch border so it does not touch either side of the pan. Repeat the process one more time, ending with the batter. Bake for 55 to 60 minutes, or until cake tester inserted into center of cake comes out clean. Cover cake with waxed paper and cool on a cake rack. When cake is cool, remove from pan and store in an airtight container.

Nutritional analysis per serving:

109	Calories	8 %	Calories from Fat
2 g	Protein	2 g	Fiber
23 g	Carbohydrates	65 mg	Sodium
1 g	Fat	0 mg	Cholesterol

Blueberry Sour Cream Coffee Cake

Indulging in this sensational, lowfat coffee cake is the perfect way to start the morning.

16 servings

Cinnamon Filling
1/3 cup firmly packed dark brown sugar
2 tablespoons granulated sugar
1 teaspoon cinnamon

Sour Cream Cake
2 cups unbleached flour
1 cup granulated sugar
1 teaspoon *each* baking soda and baking powder
1/4 teaspoon salt
1 cup nonfat sour cream
1 jar (6 ounces) pear baby food
1/2 cup egg substitute
2 teaspoons vanilla
1 cup fresh blueberries

Preheat oven to 350 degrees.

To make cinnamon filling: Combine brown sugar, 2 tablespoons sugar, and cinnamon in a small bowl. Set aside.

To make sour cream cake: Combine flour, 1 cup sugar, baking soda, baking powder, and salt in a large mixing bowl.
    Combine sour cream, pears, egg substitute, and vanilla in a small bowl and blend well. Add sour cream mixture to dry ingredients and mix with a fork until blended. Spread one-third of the batter into a 9-inch square cake pan that has been coated with vegetable spray. Sprinkle half of the cinnamon filling over batter;

repeat the process one more time, ending with the batter. Sprinkle blueberries over cake and gently press down on them with the back of a spoon so that only the tops of the blueberries show. Bake for 45 to 50 minutes, or until a cake tester inserted into the center of the cake comes out clean. Cool cake before cutting into serving pieces.

Nutritional analysis per serving:

Filling:

23	Calories	0 %	Calories from Fat
0 g	Protein	0 g	Fiber
6 g	Carbohydrates	1 mg	Sodium
0 g	Fat	0 mg	Cholesterol

Cake:

119	Calories	3 %	Calories from Fat
3 g	Protein	2 g	Fiber
26 g	Carbohydrates	127 mg	Sodium
0 g	Fat	0 mg	Cholesterol

Total:

142	Calories	2 %	Calories from Fat
3 g	Protein	2 g	Fiber
32 g	Carbohydrates	128 mg	Sodium
0 g	Fat	0 mg	Cholesterol

Sweet Breads and Coffee Cakes

Chocolate and Walnut Coffee Cake

This sensational coffee cake is chock-full of good things to eat. It can be enjoyed during a coffee break or after a rich meal, and it makes a wonderful gift when wrapped in decorative foil and tied with a colorful ribbon.

24 servings

3 cups unbleached flour
3/4 cup granulated sugar
1 1/2 teaspoons *each* baking soda and baking powder
1/4 teaspoon salt
1/2 cup *each* raisins and firmly packed dark brown sugar
1/2 cup chopped walnuts
2 tablespoons cocoa
1 tablespoon cinnamon
2 teaspoons powdered instant coffee
2 cups plain nonfat yogurt
1/2 cup prune lekvar
1 tablespoon vanilla
3 egg whites
Powdered sugar to dust cake

Preheat oven to 350 degrees.

Combine flour, sugar, baking soda, baking powder, salt, raisins, brown sugar, walnuts, cocoa, cinnamon, and coffee in a large mixing bowl.

Combine yogurt, lekvar, vanilla, and egg whites in a small bowl and blend well. Add lekvar mixture to dry ingredients and mix with a fork until blended. Spoon batter into a 10-inch Bundt pan that has been coated with vegetable spray and bake for 45 minutes, or until cake tester inserted into center of cake comes out clean. Cover cake with waxed paper and cool on a cake rack. Remove cake from pan and store in an airtight container. Dust with powdered sugar before serving.

Nutritional analysis per serving:

156	Calories	11 %	Calories from Fat
4 g	Protein	1 g	Fiber
31 g	Carbohydrates	124 mg	Sodium
2 g	Fat	0 mg	Cholesterol

Chocolate Chip Date Cake ✓

Dates and prunes are rich in fiber and nutrients. When they are combined with chocolate chips, the end result is a sweet cake that is very moist and nutritious.

16 servings

7 ounces (about 1¹/8 cups) chopped dates
1 teaspoon baking soda
1 cup boiling water
1 cup prune lekvar
2 egg whites
1 teaspoon vanilla
1³/4 cups unbleached flour
³/4 cup sugar
2 tablespoons cocoa
¹/4 teaspoon salt
¹/2 cup chocolate chips
Powdered sugar to dust cake

Preheat oven to 350 degrees.

Combine dates, baking soda, and boiling water in a medium-size mixing bowl. Let dates stand for 10 minutes or until soft. Place date mixture in work bowl of food processor and purée. Add lekvar, egg whites, and vanilla and process until smooth. Set aside.

Combine flour, sugar, cocoa, salt, and chocolate chips in a large mixing bowl.

Add date mixture to dry ingredients and mix with a fork until blended. Pour batter into a 9 × 13-inch baking pan that has been coated with vegetable spray and bake for 45 minutes, or until cake tester inserted into center of cake comes out clean. Cover cake with waxed paper and cool on a cake rack. Store in an airtight container. Dust cake lightly with powdered sugar before serving.

Nutritional analysis per serving:

192	Calories	10 %	Calories from Fat
2 g	Protein	3 g	Fiber
42 g	Carbohydrates	108 mg	Sodium
2 g	Fat	0 mg	Cholesterol

Chocolate-Glazed Marble Cake

Years ago my mother taught me this technique for marbelizing cakes. The chocolate and white batters bake into an evenly swirled cake that is spectacular to look at and delicious to eat. The cake is best when allowed to sit for at least 24 hours before glazing. It can also be served with a light dusting of powdered sugar.

21 servings

Marble Cake
1 1/2 ounces unsweetened chocolate, chopped
1 tablespoon honey
1 teaspoon powdered instant coffee
2 tablespoons water
2 1/3 cups unbleached flour
1 tablespoon baking powder
1/8 teaspoon salt
1 cup sugar
1 jar (6 ounces) pear baby food
4 egg whites
1 tablespoon vanilla
3/4 cup skim milk

Chocolate Glaze
1/2 cup chocolate chips
2 tablespoons nondairy creamer
1 teaspoon corn syrup
1/2 teaspoon vanilla

Preheat oven to 350 degrees.

To make marble cake: Place chocolate, honey, coffee, and water in a small heavy saucepan, covered, over low heat. Cook until chocolate is soft enough to blend. Set aside.

Combine flour, baking powder, salt, and sugar in a large bowl.

Combine pears, egg whites, vanilla, and milk in a medium-size bowl and blend well. Add pear mixture to dry ingredients and stir with a fork until blended. Remove 1 cup of the batter and blend with the chocolate mixture.

Coat an 8-inch Bundt pan with vegetable spray. Onto the bottom of the pan, spoon 4 dollops of chocolate batter equally spaced from one another, leaving room for 4 equal-size dollops of white batter between them. Now place 4 similar-size dollops of white batter into the spaces left between the chocolate. A total of 8 dollops, alternating white with chocolate, should now be in the pan. For the next layer, place a dollop of white batter on each chocolate dollop and a dollop of chocolate batter on each white dollop. Repeat this process until all of the batter is used. Bake for 45 to 50 minutes, or until cake tester inserted into center of cake comes out clean. Cover cake with waxed paper and cool on a cake rack. Remove cake from pan when cool.

To make chocolate glaze: Combine chocolate chips, creamer, corn syrup, and vanilla in a small heavy saucepan, covered, over low heat. Cook just until chocolate is soft enough to blend. Blend well and spoon over top of cooled cake, letting it run down the sides.

Nutritional analysis per serving:

Cake:

113	Calories	8 %	Calories from Fat
3 g	Protein	1 g	Fiber
23 g	Carbohydrates	70 mg	Sodium
1 g	Fat	1 mg	Cholesterol

Glaze:

30	Calories	60 %	Calories from Fat
0 g	Protein	1 g	Fiber
3 g	Carbohydrates	2 mg	Sodium
2 g	Fat	0 mg	Cholesterol

Total:

143	Calories	19 %	Calories from Fat
3 g	Protein	1 g	Fiber
26 g	Carbohydrates	71 mg	Sodium
3 g	Fat	1 mg	Cholesterol

Chocolate Tea Bread

This is an exceptionally moist, dense bread with an intense chocolate flavor and a subtle hint of coffee.

10 servings

1½ cups unbleached flour
¾ cup sugar
½ cup Dutch process cocoa
2 tablespoons powdered instant coffee
1½ teaspoons baking soda
⅛ teaspoon salt
5 tablespoons prune lekvar
1 cup plain nonfat yogurt
1 egg white

Preheat oven to 350 degrees.

Combine flour, sugar, cocoa, coffee, baking soda, and salt in a large mixing bowl.

Combine lekvar, yogurt, and egg white in a small bowl and blend well. Add lekvar mixture to dry ingredients and mix with a fork until blended. Spoon batter into a 9 × 5-inch loaf pan that has been coated with vegetable spray. Bake for 45 to 50 minutes, or until cake tester inserted into center of bread comes out clean. Cover bread with waxed paper and cool on a cake rack. When cool, remove bread from pan and store in an airtight container.

Nutritional analysis per serving:

172	Calories	5 %	Calories from Fat
4 g	Protein	2 g	Fiber
38 g	Carbohydrates	209 mg	Sodium
.1 g	Fat	0 mg	Cholesterol

Coffee Coffee Cake

Coffee is the dominant flavor in this moist coffee cake, hence its name. It can be topped with the coffee glaze or lightly sprinkled with powdered sugar.

21 servings

Cake
2 cups unbleached flour
1 cup granulated sugar
1 teaspoon baking powder
1/2 teaspoon baking soda
1/4 teaspoon salt
1 jar (6 ounces) pear baby food
1 cup light sour cream
2 egg whites
2 teaspoons vanilla
2 tablespoons powdered instant coffee dissolved in
    1 tablespoon hot water

Coffee Glaze
3/4 cup powdered sugar
1 to 2 tablespoons strong coffee

Preheat oven to 350 degrees.

To make cake: Combine flour, sugar, baking powder, baking soda, and salt in a large mixing bowl.

Combine pears, sour cream, egg whites, and vanilla in a small bowl and blend well. Add pear mixture to dry ingredients and mix with a fork until blended. Remove one-third of the batter to a small bowl and add the dissolved coffee. Blend well.

Spoon half of the remaining batter into a 9-inch Bundt pan that has been coated with vegetable spray. Spoon the coffee batter over the first layer, then top with the last half of the batter. Bake for 30 minutes, or until cake tester inserted into center of cake comes out clean.

Cover cake with waxed paper and cool on a cake rack for 25 minutes. Remove cake from pan, recover with waxed paper, and cool completely.

To make coffee glaze: Combine powdered sugar and just enough coffee to make a smooth glaze. Drizzle over cake one hour before serving.

2 points

Nutritional analysis per serving:

Cake:

96	Calories	10 %	Calories from Fat
2 g	Protein	1 g	Fiber
19 g	Carbohydrates	82 mg	Sodium
1 g	Fat	0 mg	Cholesterol

Glaze:

14	Calories	0 %	Calories from Fat
0 g	Protein	0 g	Fiber
4 g	Carbohydrates	0 mg	Sodium
0 g	Fat	0 mg	Cholesterol

Total:

110	Calories	10 %	Calories from Fat
2 g	Protein	1 g	Fiber
23 g	Carbohydrates	82 mg	Sodium
1 g	Fat	0 mg	Cholesterol

Cranberry Pumpkin Bread

This is the kind of hearty bread I like to make in the fall. The cranberries and pumpkin combine to make an exceptionally moist and flavorful bread.

10 servings per loaf

3 1/2 cups unbleached flour
1 2/3 cups sugar
1/2 cup chopped walnuts
2 teaspoons baking soda
1 teaspoon baking powder
1 1/2 teaspoons cinnamon
1/2 teaspoon allspice
1/4 teaspoon *each* ginger and nutmeg
1/8 teaspoon ground cloves
1/8 teaspoon salt
1 can (16 ounces) whole-berry cranberry sauce
1 can (16 ounces) solid-pack pumpkin
2/3 cup prune lekvar
4 egg whites

Preheat oven to 350 degrees.

Combine flour, sugar, walnuts, baking soda, baking powder, cinnamon, allspice, ginger, nutmeg, cloves, and salt in a large bowl.

Combine cranberry sauce, pumpkin, lekvar, and egg whites in a medium-size mixing bowl and blend until smooth. Add cranberry mixture to dry ingredients and mix with a fork until blended. Pour batter into two 9 × 5-inch loaf pans that have been coated with vegetable spray. Bake for 65 to 70 minutes, or until cake tester inserted into center of bread comes out clean. Cool breads in pans for 5 minutes. Remove breads from pans, cover with waxed paper, and cool on cake racks. Store in airtight containers.

3 pts

Nutritional analysis per serving:

222	Calories	9 %	Calories from Fat
4 g	Protein	4 g	Fiber
49 g	Carbohydrates	135 mg	Sodium
2 g	Fat	0 mg	Cholesterol

Georgia's Apple Coffee Cake

This recipe was given to me by my friend Georgia. The fusion of spices and thinly sliced apples produces a deliciously moist cake. It is the ideal dessert to enjoy on an autumn day or as a light finale to a rich dinner.

18 servings

2 cups unbleached flour
1 cup *each* granulated sugar and firmly packed
    dark brown sugar
2 teaspoons baking powder
1 teaspoon *each* cinnamon and nutmeg
1/2 teaspoon baking soda
1/4 teaspoon salt
1 jar (6 ounces) applesauce baby food
1 cup buttermilk
2 egg whites
4 Red Delicious apples, peeled, cored, and thinly sliced

Preheat oven to 350 degrees.

Combine flour, sugars, baking powder, cinnamon, nutmeg, baking soda, and salt in a large mixing bowl.

Combine applesauce, buttermilk, and egg whites in a small mixing bowl and blend until smooth. Add applesauce mixture to dry ingredients and mix with a fork until blended. Spoon batter into a 9 × 13-inch baking pan that has been coated with vegetable spray. Gently press sliced apples into top of batter and bake for 45 minutes, or until cake tester inserted into center of cake comes out clean.

162	Calories	2 %	Calories from Fat
2 g	Protein	1 g	Fiber
38 g	Carbohydrates	109 mg	Sodium
0 g	Fat	1 mg	Cholesterol

Hazelnut Coffee Cake

The boldness of the spices harmonizing with the hazelnuts and chocolate chips in this coffee cake are a welcome delight first thing in the morning. Serve with a pot of steaming coffee or tea.

16 servings

1 cup hazelnuts
1/2 cup chocolate chips
2 1/2 cups unbleached flour
2 cups powdered sugar
2 teaspoons baking powder
2 teaspoons ground cinnamon
1/2 teaspoon ground cloves
1/2 cup chopped dates
1 jar (6 ounces) pear baby food
4 egg whites
1/2 cup skim milk
2 teaspoons vanilla
Powdered sugar to dust cake

Preheat oven to 350 degrees.

Place hazelnuts in a small pan and bake for 12 minutes. Set aside.

In work bowl of food processor, process chocolate chips until coarsely chopped. Add hazelnuts and process until finely chopped.

Combine flour, sugar, baking powder, cinnamon, cloves, dates, and chocolate-hazelnut mixture in a large mixing bowl.

Combine pears, egg whites, milk, and vanilla in a small bowl and blend well. Add pear mixture to dry ingredients and mix with a fork until blended. Spoon batter into an 8 × 11.5 × 2-inch oblong baking dish that has been coated with vegetable spray and bake for 30 to 35 minutes, or until cake tester inserted into center of cake comes out clean. Cover cake with waxed paper and cool on a cake rack. When cake is cool, cut into squares and store in an airtight container. Dust with powdered sugar before serving.

Nutritional analysis per serving:

219	Calories	30 %	Calories from Fat
5 g	Protein	4 g	Fiber
35 g	Carbohydrates	62 mg	Sodium
8 g	Fat	1 mg	Cholesterol

Healthful Apple Cake

This apple cake is made with a cornucopia of wholesome foods. Apples, raisins, bran cereal, and yogurt combine to create a cake that is not only good for you but satisfying to eat.

24 servings

1 1/2 cups whole wheat flour
1 cup 100% bran cereal
1/2 cup firmly packed dark brown sugar
1 1/2 teaspoons cinnamon
1 teaspoon baking soda
1/8 teaspoon salt
1/2 cup raisins
1 jar (6 ounces) applesauce baby food
1 cup plain nonfat yogurt
1 tablespoon honey
3 egg whites
2 apples, peeled, cored, and chopped
1 tablespoon vanilla

Preheat oven to 350 degrees.

Combine flour, cereal, brown sugar, cinnamon, baking soda, salt, and raisins in a large mixing bowl.

Combine applesauce, yogurt, honey, egg whites, apples, and vanilla in a medium-size bowl and blend well. Add apple mixture to dry ingredients and mix with a fork until blended. Spoon batter into an 8 × 11.5 × 2-inch oblong baking dish that has been coated with vegetable spray and bake for 35 to 45 minutes, or until cake tester inserted into center of cake comes out clean. Cool cake before cutting into squares.

Nutritional analysis per serving:

83	Calories	5 %	Calories from Fat
3 g	Protein	2 g	Fiber
19 g	Carbohydrates	62 mg	Sodium
1 g	Fat	0 mg	Cholesterol

Holiday Honey Cake

Honey cake is traditionally served on Rosh Hashana, the Jewish New Year. The sweetness of the honey represents hope for the beginning of a sweet and good year.

10 servings

2 ¼ cups unbleached flour
¾ cup firmly packed dark brown sugar
2 teaspoons cinnamon
¾ teaspoon *each* baking soda and baking powder
¼ teaspoon salt
1 cup coarsely chopped walnuts
3 tablespoons prune lekvar
¾ cup strong coffee
¾ cup honey
3 egg whites
2 tablespoons finely grated orange peel

Preheat oven to 350 degrees.

Combine flour, brown sugar, cinnamon, baking soda, baking powder, salt, and walnuts in a large mixing bowl.

Combine lekvar, coffee, honey, egg whites, and orange peel in a small bowl and blend well. Add honey mixture to dry ingredients and mix with a fork until blended. Spoon batter into a 9 × 5-inch loaf pan that has been coated with vegetable spray and bake for 65 to 75 minutes, or until cake tester inserted into center of cake comes out clean. Cover cake with waxed paper and cool on a cake rack. When cake is cool, remove from pan and store in an airtight container.

Nutritional analysis per serving:

338	Calories	20 %	Calories from Fat
6 g	Protein	2 g	Fiber
64 g	Carbohydrates	165 mg	Sodium
8 g	Fat	0 mg	Cholesterol

Italian Raisin Cake

A spectacular cake studded with raisins and bursting with flavor.

24 servings

4 cups unbleached flour
2 cups sugar
2 tablespoons baking powder
1 cup raisins
1 jar (6 ounces) pear baby food
6 egg whites
1 cup orange juice
1 teaspoon finely grated orange peel
Powdered sugar to dust cake

Preheat oven to 350 degrees.

Combine flour, sugar, baking powder, and raisins in a large mixing bowl.

Combine pears, egg whites, orange juice, and orange peel in a small bowl and blend well. Add pear mixture to dry ingredients and mix with a fork until blended. Spoon batter into a 10-inch Bundt pan that has been coated with vegetable spray. Bake for 35 to 45 minutes, or until cake tester inserted into cake comes out clean. Cover cake with waxed paper and cool on a cake rack for 20 minutes. Remove cake from pan, recover with waxed paper, and cool completely. Store in an airtight container. Dust cake with powdered sugar before serving.

Nutritional analysis per serving:

174	Calories	2 %	Calories from Fat
3 g	Protein	1 g	Fiber
40 g	Carbohydrates	88 mg	Sodium
0 g	Fat	0 mg	Cholesterol

Lowfat Carrot Cake

This recipe appears courtesy of the California Prune Board.

12 servings

4 cups grated carrots (spooned, not packed into cup)
2 cups sugar
1 can (8 ounces) crushed pineapple
1 cup prune lekvar or prune butter (see Helpful Hints)
4 egg whites
2 teaspoons vanilla
2 cups unbleached flour
2 teaspoons baking soda
2 teaspoons cinnamon
$1/2$ teaspoon salt
$3/4$ cup shredded or flaked coconut

Preheat oven to 375 degrees.

Combine carrots, sugar, pineapple, lekvar, egg whites, and vanilla in a medium-size bowl and blend well.

Combine flour, baking soda, cinnamon, salt, and coconut in a large mixing bowl. Add carrot mixture to dry ingredients and mix with a fork until blended. Spoon batter into a 9 × 13-inch pan that has been coated with vegetable spray and bake for about 45 minutes, or until a cake tester inserted into center of cake comes out clean. Cool on rack. Cut into 3 × 3 1/4-inch squares.

Nutritional analysis per serving:

304	Calories	5 %	Calories from Fat
4 g	Protein	2 g	Fiber
88 g	Carbohydrates	276 mg	Sodium
2g	Fat	0 mg	Cholesterol

Sweet Breads and Coffee Cakes

Lowfat Prune-Pecan Bread

This recipe appears courtesy of the California Prune Board.

24 servings

3/4 cup prune lekvar or prune butter (see Helpful Hints)
3/4 cup prune juice
2 teaspoons finely grated orange peel
1 cup toasted wheat germ
3/4 cup whole wheat flour
1/2 cup unbleached flour
2/3 cup firmly packed dark brown sugar
1 teaspoon baking powder
1/2 teaspoon baking soda
1/2 teaspoon salt
1/2 cup chopped pecans
2 egg whites

Preheat oven to 350 degrees.

Combine lekvar, prune juice, and orange peel in a saucepan over moderate heat and bring just to a boil. Remove from heat and set aside.

Combine wheat germ, flours, sugar, baking powder, baking soda, salt, and pecans in a large mixing bowl. Add egg whites and prune mixture to dry ingredients and mix with a fork until blended. Spoon batter into an 8 1/2 × 4 1/2-inch loaf pan that has been coated with vegetable spray and bake for about 50 minutes, or until cake tester inserted into center of bread comes out clean. Cool in pan 10 minutes. Turn bread onto rack to cool completely.

Nutritional analysis per serving:

92	Calories	20 %	Calories from Fat
3 g	Protein	2 g	Fiber
17 g	Carbohydrates	83 mg	Sodium
2 g	Fat	0 mg	Cholesterol

Sweet Breads and Coffee Cakes

Mocha Cake

This impressive coffee cake can be served as a light dessert with fresh berries or topped with a dollop of nonfat whipped cream.

21 servings

2 cups unbleached flour
3/4 cup sugar
1/2 cup Dutch process cocoa
2 tablespoons powdered instant coffee
1/2 teaspoon baking soda
1/4 teaspoon salt
1/2 cup prune lekvar
3 egg whites
1/4 cup coffee liqueur
2/3 cup skim milk
2 tablespoons honey
1 tablespoon vanilla
Powdered sugar to dust cake

Preheat oven to 325 degrees.

Combine flour, sugar, cocoa, coffee, baking soda, and salt in a large mixing bowl.

Combine lekvar and egg whites in a small bowl and blend well. Add liqueur, milk, honey, and vanilla and blend well. Add lekvar mixture to dry ingredients and mix with a fork until blended. Spoon batter into a 9-inch Bundt pan that has been coated with vegetable spray. Bake for 50 to 55 minutes, or until cake tester inserted into center of cake comes out clean. Cover cake with waxed paper and cool on cake rack. When cake is cool, remove from pan and store in an airtight container. Dust cake with powdered sugar before serving.

Nutritional analysis per serving:

118	Calories	4 %	Calories from Fat
2 g	Protein	1 g	Fiber
25 g	Carbohydrates	76 mg	Sodium
1 g	Fat	0 mg	Cholesterol

Sweet Breads and Coffee Cakes

Old-Fashioned Gingerbread

Gingerbread has been an all-time favorite dessert of young and old alike. It is sweet and spicy and tastes delicious when topped with a small dollop of nonfat whipped cream or frozen yogurt.

16 servings

2 1/4 cups unbleached flour
3/4 cup firmly packed dark brown sugar
1 1/2 teaspoons *each* ginger and cinnamon
1/2 teaspoon *each* nutmeg and ground cloves
1/4 teaspoon allspice
2 teaspoons baking powder
1/2 teaspoon baking soda
1/8 teaspoon salt
1 cup water
3/4 cup prune lekvar
2 egg whites
3/4 cup molasses

Preheat oven to 350 degrees.

Combine flour, brown sugar, ginger, cinnamon, nutmeg, cloves, allspice, baking powder, baking soda, and salt in a large mixing bowl.

Combine water, lekvar, egg whites, and molasses in a small bowl and blend well. Add lekvar mixture to dry ingredients and mix with a fork until blended. Spoon batter into a 9 × 13-inch pan that has been coated with vegetable spray. Bake for 35 minutes, or until cake tester inserted into center of gingerbread comes out clean. When gingerbread is cool, cover with plastic wrap. Cut into squares before serving.

Nutritional analysis per serving:

169	Calories	1 %	Calories from Fat
2 g	Protein	1 g	Fiber
40 g	Carbohydrates	99 mg	Sodium
0 g	Fat	0 mg	Cholesterol

Pear Coffee Cake

3pts ✓

This coffee cake tastes almost like pear pie. Serve it plain with just a dusting of powdered sugar or with a scoop of nonfat frozen yogurt.

8 servings

1 cup unbleached flour
3/4 cup sugar
1/2 teaspoon baking powder
1/4 teaspoon baking soda
1 teaspoon cinnamon
1/2 teaspoon *each* nutmeg and ginger
1/8 teaspoon allspice
1/8 teaspoon salt
1/4 cup pear baby food
1 egg white
1 1/2 pounds pears, thinly sliced

Preheat oven to 350 degrees.

Combine flour, sugar, baking powder, baking soda, cinnamon, nutmeg, ginger, allspice, and salt in a large mixing bowl.

Combine pear baby food and egg whites in a small bowl and blend well. Add pear mixture to dry ingredients and mix with a fork until blended. Add sliced pears and mix until they are coated with batter. Spoon mixture into a 9-inch pie pan that has been coated with vegetable spray. Bake for 50 minutes. Serve while still warm or at room temperature.

181	Calories	5 %	Calories from Fat
2 g	Protein	2 g	Fiber
41 g	Carbohydrates	98 mg	Sodium
1 g	Fat	0 mg	Cholesterol

Pineapple Tea Bread

This is a delicious, old-fashioned pineapple bread that tastes best when allowed to sit for 24 hours.

10 servings

2 cups unbleached flour
1 cup sugar
1/2 cup walnuts (optional)
2 teaspoons baking powder
1/2 teaspoon baking soda
1/2 teaspoon mace
1/4 teaspoon salt
1 egg white
1 can (8 ounces) crushed pineapple
1/2 cup skim milk
1/4 cup pear-pineapple baby food

Preheat oven to 350 degrees.

Combine flour, sugar, walnuts, baking powder, baking soda, mace, and salt in a large mixing bowl.

Combine egg white, pineapple, milk, and pear-pineapple in a medium-size bowl and blend well. Add pineapple mixture to dry ingredients and mix with a fork until blended. Spoon batter into a 9 × 5-inch loaf pan that has been coated with vegetable spray. Bake for 45 to 50 minutes. Cover bread with waxed paper and cool in pan on a cake rack for 20 minutes. Remove bread from pan, recover with waxed paper, and cool completely. Store in an airtight container.

Nutritional analysis per serving:

Bread with walnuts:

236	Calories	15 %	Calories from Fat
4 g	Protein	1 g	Fiber
47 g	Carbohydrates	148 mg	Sodium
4 g	Fat	0 mg	Cholesterol

Bread without walnuts:

197	Calories	1 %	Calories from Fat
3 g	Protein	1 g	Fiber
46 g	Carbohydrates	147 mg	Sodium
0 g	Fat	0 mg	Cholesterol

Poppy Seed and Cinnamon Cake

The merger of cinnamon and poppy seeds produces a unique bread. It can be iced with a cinnamon glaze or lightly dusted with powdered sugar before serving.

21 servings

1/4 cup sugar
1 teaspoon cinnamon
2 1/2 cups unbleached flour
1 cup sugar
1 teaspoon *each* baking powder and baking soda
1/8 teaspoon salt
3 tablespoons poppy seeds
1 jar (6 ounces) pear baby food
1 cup buttermilk
1/2 cup egg substitute
2 egg whites
1/2 teaspoon *each* butter flavoring and vanilla

Preheat oven to 350 degrees.

Combine 1/4 cup sugar and 1 teaspoon cinnamon in a small bowl. Set aside.

Combine flour, 1 cup sugar, baking powder, baking soda, salt, and poppy seeds in a large mixing bowl.

Combine pears, buttermilk, egg substitute, egg whites, butter flavoring, and vanilla in a small bowl and blend well. Add pear mixture to dry ingredients and mix with a fork until blended. Spoon one-third of the batter into a 9-inch Bundt pan that has been coated with vegetable spray. Spoon one-half of the cinnamon-sugar mixture over batter; repeat process one more time, ending with batter. Bake for 55 minutes, or until cake tester inserted into center of cake comes out clean. Cover cake with waxed paper and cool on a cake rack. When cake is cool, remove from pan and store cake in an airtight container. The cake tastes best if allowed to sit for 24 hours.

Note: To make a cinnamon glaze, mix 1/2 cup powdered sugar, scant 1/2 teaspoon cinnamon, 1 1/2 teaspoons skim milk, and 1/2 teaspoon butter flavoring; blend until smooth. Spoon glaze over cake. The glaze remains as a firm coating on the cake for several hours. Soon after, the glaze is absorbed into the cake, which adds to its flavor.

Nutritional analysis per serving:

117	Calories	8 %	Calories from Fat
3 g	Protein	2 g	Fiber
24 g	Carbohydrates	92 mg	Sodium
1 g	Fat	0 mg	Cholesterol

Pumpkin, Raisin, and Walnut Bread

My favorite time of the year to make this hearty bread is in the fall.

10 servings

1 2/3 cups unbleached flour
1 1/4 cups sugar
1 teaspoon baking soda
1 teaspoon cinnamon
1/2 teaspoon ground cloves
1/2 teaspoon *each* salt and baking powder
1/3 cup chopped walnuts
1/3 cup raisins
1 cup solid-pack canned pumpkin
1/3 cup prune lekvar
2 egg whites
2 tablespoons water
1 teaspoon vanilla

Preheat oven to 350 degrees.

Combine flour, sugar, baking soda, cinnamon, cloves, salt, baking powder, walnuts, and raisins in a large mixing bowl.

Combine pumpkin, lekvar, egg whites, water, and vanilla in a small bowl and blend well. Add pumpkin mixture to dry ingredients and mix with a fork until blended. Spoon batter into a 9 × 5-inch loaf pan that has been coated with vegetable spray. Bake for 50 minutes, or until cake tester inserted into center of bread comes out clean. Cover bread with waxed paper and cool on a cake rack. When bread is cool, store in an airtight container.

Nutritional analysis per serving:

221	Calories	11 %	Calories from Fat
4 g	Protein	4 g	Fiber
47 g	Carbohydrates	218 mg	Sodium
3 g	Fat	0 mg	Cholesterol

Sweet Breads and Coffee Cakes

Rhubarb Cake Squares

Although most people think of rhubarb as a fruit, it is really a vegetable. Rhubarb is exceptionally tasty in this cake . . . not too sweet, and its flavor lingers long after the first bite.

16 squares

1 pound fresh rhubarb, washed, stems removed
  and sliced into 1/4-inch slices
1 cup sugar
1 cup *each* unbleached and whole wheat flours
1 teaspoon baking soda
1/8 teaspoon salt
1 teaspoon cinnamon
1 jar (6 ounces) pear baby food
1 cup plain nonfat yogurt
2 egg whites
2 teaspoons vanilla

Place rhubarb in a large glass bowl and sprinkle with sugar. Let sit for 30 minutes.

Preheat oven to 325 degrees.

Combine flours, baking soda, salt, and cinnamon in a large mixing bowl.

Combine pears, yogurt, egg whites, and vanilla in a small bowl; add to rhubarb and blend well. Add rhubarb mixture to dry ingredients and mix with a fork until blended. Spoon batter into an 8 × 11.5 × 2-inch oblong baking dish that has been coated with vegetable spray and bake for 40 minutes, or until a cake tester inserted into center of cake comes out clean. Cover with waxed paper and cool on a cake rack. When cool, cut into squares and store in an airtight container.

Nutritional analysis per square:

125	Calories	3 %	Calories from Fat
4 g	Protein	3 g	Fiber
27 g	Carbohydrates	88 mg	Sodium
1 g	Fat	0 mg	Cholesterol

Sour Cream Coffee Cake

Sour cream coffee cake is a celebrated delight often served at brunch or morning coffee. This flavorsome cake is exceptionally moist and is sure to become a favorite. Dust top of cake with powdered sugar before serving.

21 servings

Cinnamon Filling
¹/₄ cup firmly packed dark brown sugar
2 tablespoons granulated sugar
3 tablespoons raisins
2 teaspoons cinnamon

Cake
2 cups unbleached flour
1 cup granulated sugar
1 teaspoon *each* baking soda and baking powder
¹/₂ teaspoon salt
1 jar (6 ounces) pear baby food
1 cup nonfat sour cream
¹/₂ cup egg substitute
2 teaspoons vanilla

Preheat oven to 350 degrees.

To make cinnamon filling: Combine sugars, raisins, and cinnamon in a small bowl and blend well. Set aside.

To make cake: Combine flour, granulated sugar, baking soda, baking powder, and salt in a large mixing bowl.

Combine pears, sour cream, egg substitute, and vanilla in a small bowl and mix well. Add sour cream mixture to dry ingredients and mix with a fork until blended. Spread a thin layer of batter into an 8-inch Bundt pan that has been coated with vegetable spray. Sprinkle half of the cinnamon filling over batter; repeat this process one more time, ending with batter. Bake for 45 to 50 minutes, or until cake tester inserted into center of cake comes out clean. Cover cake with waxed paper and cool on a cake rack for 25 minutes. Remove cake from pan, recover with waxed paper, and cool completely. Store in an airtight container.

Nutritional analysis per serving:

Cake:

95	Calories	2 %	Calories from Fat
2 g	Protein	0 g	Fiber
21 g	Carbohydrates	121 mg	Sodium
0 g	Fat	0 mg	Cholesterol

Filling:

19	Calories	15 %	Calories from Fat
0 g	Protein	0 g	Fiber
5 g	Carbohydrates	1 mg	Sodium
0 g	Fat	0 mg	Cholesterol

Total:

114	Calories	1 %	Calories from Fat
2 g	Protein	0 g	Fiber
26 g	Carbohydrates	122 mg	Sodium
0 g	Fat	0 mg	Cholesterol

Sweet Breads and Coffee Cakes

Southwestern Pound Cake

A not-too-sweet cake that is delicious when sprinkled with powdered sugar and served with fresh strawberries, blueberries, or raspberries.

16 servings

1 1/2 cups unbleached flour
3/4 cup cornmeal
1 teaspoon baking powder
4 ounces almond paste
1 jar (6 ounces) pear baby food
1 1/4 cups sugar
1 cup frozen nondairy whipping cream, defrosted
6 egg whites
1 teaspoon vanilla

Preheat oven to 350 degrees.

Combine flour, cornmeal, and baking powder in a large mixing bowl.

In work bowl of food processor, process almond paste, pears, and sugar until smooth. Add whipping cream, egg whites, and vanilla; process until smooth. Add almond paste mixture to dry ingredients and mix with a fork until blended. Pour batter into a 9-inch square baking pan that has been coated with vegetable spray. Bake for 30 minutes, or until cake tester inserted into center of cake comes out clean. Cover cake with waxed paper and cool on a cake rack before cutting into squares. Store in an airtight container.

Nutritional analysis per serving:

205	Calories	27 %	Calories from Fat
4 g	Protein	3 g	Fiber
35 g	Carbohydrates	55 mg	Sodium
6 g	Fat	0 mg	Cholesterol

Spiced Pumpkin Bread

After a day of skiing or sledding, this spicy bread is especially good when served with a cup of steaming hot apple cider. It is dense, moist, and delicious. For added nutrition and texture, add a cup of raisins or chopped dates to the batter before baking.

10 servings

1 2/3 cups unbleached flour
1 1/2 cups sugar
1 teaspoon baking soda
1/4 teaspoon baking powder
1/4 teaspoon salt
1 teaspoon cinnamon
1/2 teaspoon *each* ground cloves and nutmeg
1/4 teaspoon allspice
1 1/4 cups solid-pack canned pumpkin
1/2 cup prune lekvar
1/2 cup orange juice
2 egg whites

Preheat oven to 350 degrees.

Combine flour, sugar, baking soda, baking powder, salt, cinnamon, cloves, nutmeg, and allspice in a large mixing bowl.

Combine pumpkin, lekvar, orange juice, and egg whites in a small bowl and blend well. Add pumpkin mixture to dry ingredients and mix with a fork until blended. Spoon batter into a 9 × 5-inch loaf pan that has been coated with vegetable spray. Bake for 70 to 75 minutes, or until cake tester inserted into center of bread comes out clean. Cover bread with waxed paper and cool on a cake rack for 25 minutes. Remove bread from pan, recover with waxed paper, and cool completely. Store in an airtight container.

Nutritional analysis per serving:

236	Calories	2 %	Calories from Fat
4 g	Protein	4 g	Fiber
57 g	Carbohydrates	166 mg	Sodium
1 g	Fat	0 mg	Cholesterol

Tipsy Chocolate Cake

This cake has just a hint of bourbon flavor, which combines wonderfully with the chocolate and prune lekvar to produce a flavorful dense cake. It can be served after a savory dinner or as an addition to a brunch buffet.

24 servings

5 ounces unsweetened chocolate
2 cups unbleached flour
1 2/3 cups granulated sugar
1 teaspoon baking soda
1/4 teaspoon salt
1/2 cup boiling water
2 tablespoons powdered instant coffee
1 cup cold water
1/2 cup prune lekvar
1/2 cup bourbon
3 egg whites
2 tablespoons canola oil
1 1/2 teaspoons vanilla
Powdered sugar to dust cake

Preheat oven to 325 degrees.

Place chocolate in a small heavy saucepan. Cook, covered, over low heat, until chocolate is soft enough to blend. Set aside.

Combine flour, sugar, baking soda, and salt in a large mixing bowl.

Combine 1/2 cup boiling water and coffee in a small bowl and blend well. Add 1 cup cold water, lekvar, bourbon, egg whites, oil, vanilla, and melted chocolate; blend well. Add bourbon mixture to dry ingredients and mix with a fork until blended. Spoon batter into a 10-inch Bundt pan that has been coated with vegetable spray. Bake for 1 hour, or until cake tester inserted into center of cake comes out clean. Cover cake with waxed paper and cool on a cake rack for 25 minutes. Remove cake from pan, recover with waxed paper, and let cool completely. Store in an airtight container. When ready to serve, sprinkle top of cake with powdered sugar.

Nutritional analysis per serving:

155	Calories	20 %	Calories from Fat
2 g	Protein	1 g	Fiber
28 g	Carbohydrates	68 mg	Sodium
3 g	Fat	0 mg	Cholesterol

Yuletide Fruit and Jam Cake

During the holiday season, it is especially nice to have a variety of cakes and cookies on hand to serve to friends, family, or unexpected guests. Because the flavor of this cake fully emerges after a few days, you should plan to make it a couple of days before Christmas.

21 servings

1 1/2 cups (8 ounces) raisins
1 cup (6 ounces) chopped dates
6 tablespoons bourbon
1 1/2 cups unbleached flour
1 cup sugar
1 teaspoon *each* cinnamon and nutmeg
1/2 teaspoon allspice
1/2 teaspoon baking soda
1/4 teaspoon salt
1 jar (12 ounces) blackberry jam
1 jar (6 ounces) pear baby food
1/4 cup buttermilk
3 egg whites

Combine raisins, dates, and bourbon in a medium-size nonmetal bowl. Let sit, covered, for 6 hours or overnight.

Preheat oven to 275 degrees.

Combine flour, sugar, cinnamon, nutmeg, allspice, baking soda, and salt in a large mixing bowl.

Add jam, pears, buttermilk, and egg whites to fruit mixture and blend well. Add fruit mixture to dry ingredients and mix with a fork until blended. Spoon batter into a 9-inch Bundt pan that has been coated with vegetable spray. Bake for 1 hour and 25 minutes, or until cake tester inserted into center of cake comes out clean. Cover cake with waxed paper and cool on a cake rack. When cake is cool, remove from pan and store in an airtight container. The cake tastes best if allowed to sit for a few days.

Nutritional analysis per serving:

186	Calories	2 %	Calories from Fat
2 g	Protein	2 g	Fiber
44 g	Carbohydrates	60 mg	Sodium
0 g	Fat	0 mg	Cholesterol

Zucchini Tea Bread

When your garden is overflowing with zucchini, use your bounty to make this wonderful bread bursting with spices and flavor.

10 servings

3 cups unbleached flour
1 cup sugar
1 teaspoon baking soda
1/2 teaspoon baking powder
1/4 teaspoon salt
1 teaspoon *each* allspice and cinnamon
1 pound zucchini, washed, ends removed, and cut
        into 2-inch pieces
2 egg whites
1 jar (6 ounces) pear baby food
2 teaspoons vanilla
1 cup raisins (optional)

Preheat oven to 350 degrees.

Combine flour, sugar, baking soda, baking powder, salt, allspice, and cinnamon in a large mixing bowl.

In work bowl of food processor, process zucchini until finely chopped. Add egg whites, pears, and vanilla and blend until smooth. Add zucchini mixture to dry ingredients and mix with a fork until blended. Spoon batter into a 9 × 5-inch loaf pan that has been coated with vegetable spray. Bake for 1 hour and 10 to 15 minutes, or until cake tester inserted into center of bread comes out clean. Cover bread with waxed paper and cool on cake rack for 20 minutes. Remove bread from pan, recover with waxed paper, and cool completely. Store in an airtight container.

Note: It is best to use a serrated knife when slicing the zucchini bread.

Nutritional analysis per serving:

Bread:

229	Calories	2 %	Calories from Fat
5 g	Protein	1 g	Fiber
50 g	Carbohydrates	166 mg	Sodium
1 g	Fat	0 mg	Cholesterol

Bread with raisins:

278	Calories	2 %	Calories from Fat
5 g	Protein	2 g	Fiber
63 g	Carbohydrates	168 mg	Sodium
1 g	Fat	0 mg	Cholesterol

Cookies and Bars

Banana and Raisin Bars

These spicy fruit bars are moist, delicious, and wholesome. They can be enjoyed at any time of the day or make a special treat when tucked into a lunch box.

16 bars

2 cups unbleached flour
1/2 cup sugar
1 teaspoon baking powder
1/2 teaspoon baking soda
1/4 teaspoon salt
1 teaspoon cinnamon
1/4 teaspoon *each* nutmeg and allspice
1 cup raisins
2 ripe bananas
1 jar (6 ounces) pear baby food
2 egg whites
1/4 cup molasses

Preheat oven to 350 degrees.

Combine flour, sugar, baking powder, baking soda, salt, cinnamon, nutmeg, allspice, and raisins in a large mixing bowl.

In work bowl of food processor, process bananas until puréed. Add pears, egg whites, and molasses and process until smooth. Add banana mixture to dry ingredients and mix with a fork until blended. Spoon batter into an 8 × 11.5 × 2-inch oblong baking dish that has been coated with vegetable spray and bake for 25 to 30 minutes, or until cake tester inserted into center of cake comes out clean. Cover cake with waxed paper and cool on a cake rack. When cake is cool, cut into bars and store in an airtight container.

Nutritional analysis per bar:

141	Calories	2 %	Calories from Fat
3 g	Protein	1 g	Fiber
33 g	Carbohydrates	91 mg	Sodium
1 g	Fat	0 mg	Cholesterol

Chocolate Chip and Raisin Cookies

30 cookies

1 1/2 cups unbleached flour
2 cups crispy rice cereal
1 cup sugar
1/2 teaspoon baking soda
1/4 teaspoon salt
1 cup *each* chocolate chips and raisins
1 jar (6 ounces) pear baby food
1 egg white
1 teaspoon vanilla

Preheat oven to 350 degrees.

Combine flour, cereal, sugar, baking soda, salt, chocolate chips, and raisins in a large mixing bowl.

Combine pears, egg white, and vanilla in a small bowl and blend well. Add pear mixture to dry ingredients and mix with a fork until blended. Drop dough by the tablespoonful, 1 inch apart, onto a baking sheet that has been coated with vegetable spray. Bake for 14 to 16 minutes, or until cookies are golden. Cool. Store cookies in an airtight container.

Nutritional analysis per cookie:

106	Calories	18 %	Calories from Fat
1 g	Protein	1 g	Fiber
21 g	Carbohydrates	59 mg	Sodium
2 g	Fat	0 mg	Cholesterol

Chocolate Chip Cookies

A chocolate chip cookie and a cold glass of milk is an all-time favorite snack. These cookies are made with wheat germ and oats to provide a little extra nutrition.

30 cookies

Heaping 3/4 cup unbleached flour
3/4 cup toasted wheat germ
1/2 cup granulated sugar
1/3 cup firmly packed dark brown sugar
1/4 cup quick-cooking oats
1/4 cup chopped walnuts
1 teaspoon baking powder
1/4 teaspoon salt
1 cup chocolate chips
1 jar (6 ounces) applesauce baby food
1 egg white
1 teaspoon vanilla

Preheat oven to 350 degrees.

Combine flour, wheat germ, sugars, oats, walnuts, baking powder, salt, and chocolate chips in a large mixing bowl.

Combine applesauce, egg white, and vanilla in a small bowl and blend well. Add applesauce mixture to dry ingredients and mix with a fork until blended. Drop dough by the teaspoonful, 1 inch apart, onto baking sheets that have been coated with vegetable spray. Bake for 17 to 20 minutes, or until cookies are golden brown.

Nutritional analysis per cookie:

83	Calories	31 %	Calories from Fat
2 g	Protein	1 g	Fiber
14 g	Carbohydrates	35 mg	Sodium
3 g	Fat	0 mg	Cholesterol

Chocolate Chip Oatmeal Bars

Oats and wheat germ make these cookies a nutritious snack.

24 bars

3 cups quick-cooking oats
1 cup unbleached flour
1 1/2 cups firmly packed dark brown sugar
1/2 cup toasted wheat germ
1 teaspoon baking soda
1 cup chocolate chips
1 jar (6 ounces) pear baby food
2 egg whites
1 tablespoon vanilla

Preheat oven to 350 degrees.

Combine oats, flour, brown sugar, wheat germ, baking soda, and chocolate chips in a large mixing bowl.

Combine pears, egg whites, and vanilla in a small bowl and blend well. Add pear mixture to dry ingredients and mix with a fork until blended. Spoon batter evenly into a 9 × 13-inch baking pan that has been coated with vegetable spray and bake for 25 minutes. Cool cake before cutting into bars.

Nutritional analysis per bar:

161	Calories	19 %	Calories from Fat
3 g	Protein	2 g	Fiber
30 g	Carbohydrates	45 mg	Sodium
3 g	Fat	0 mg	Cholesterol

Chocolate-Nut Freezer Cookies

These cookies taste best when allowed to sit for 24 hours.

36 cookies

1/2 cup chocolate chips
1/2 cup pecans
2 cups unbleached flour
1/2 cup firmly packed dark brown sugar
1/4 cup granulated sugar
1/2 teaspoon baking soda
1/4 teaspoon salt
1 jar (6 ounces) pear baby food
1/2 teaspoon vanilla

In work bowl of food processor, process chocolate chips until coarsely chopped. Add pecans and process until mixture is finely chopped. Add flour, sugars, baking soda, and salt and process until blended. Transfer mixture to a large mixing bowl.

Combine pears and vanilla in a small bowl and blend well. Add pear mixture to dry ingredients and mix with a fork until just blended. Using hands, gently squeeze dough until completely blended. Place dough on a piece of plastic wrap and form into a log, about 2 inches in diameter. Wrap log in plastic wrap and freeze for 30 minutes, or until cookies are firm enough to slice.

Preheat oven to 350 degrees.

Slice cookies 1/4 inch thick and place 1 inch apart on a baking sheet that has been coated with vegetable spray. Bake for 8 to 12 minutes, or until cookies are golden brown.

Nutritional analysis per cookie:

62	Calories	28 %	Calories from Fat
1 g	Protein	0 g	Fiber
11 g	Carbohydrates	43 mg	Sodium
2 g	Fat	0 mg	Cholesterol

Christmas Fruitcake Cookies

The kaleidoscope of dried fruits in these festive and colorful holiday cookies is delicately enhanced by bourbon. The flavor improves if the cookies are allowed to sit for a couple of days.

24 cookies

3/4 cup unbleached flour
1/4 cup firmly packed dark brown sugar
3/4 teaspoon baking soda
1 teaspoon *each* allspice and cinnamon
1/2 pound mixed candied fruit (reserve 24 small pieces)
1/2 cup raisins
2 tablespoons prune lekvar
1 egg white
1/4 cup bourbon

Preheat oven to 300 degrees.

Combine flour, brown sugar, baking soda, allspice, cinnamon, candied fruit minus reserved pieces, and raisins in a large mixing bowl.

Combine lekvar, egg white, and bourbon in a small bowl and blend well. Add lekvar mixture to dry ingredients and mix with a fork until blended. Drop dough by the tablespoonful, 1 inch apart, on a baking sheet that has been coated with vegetable spray. Top each cookie with a piece of reserved candied fruit. Bake for 30 minutes. Cool cookies on a cake rack.

When cookies are cool, lightly moisten a cotton dish towel with bourbon. Place cookies in an airtight container and cover with bourbon-soaked towel.

Nutritional analysis per cookie:

83	Calories	17 %	Calories from Fat
1 g	Protein	1 g	Fiber
16 g	Carbohydrates	45 mg	Sodium
2 g	Fat	4 mg	Cholesterol

Chunky Oatmeal and Dried Fruit Cookies

The inspiration for these cookies came from one of my daughter's friends who is very health conscious. She made cookies very similar to these and they tasted delicious. I adapted her recipe by substituting pear baby food and adding additional dried fruit.

42 cookies

3 cups rolled oats
2 cups unbleached flour
1 cup sugar
1/2 cup *each* dried cranberries, raisins, and chopped dates
1/2 teaspoon *each* cinnamon and ground cloves
1 teaspoon baking soda
1/2 teaspoon baking powder
1/4 teaspoon salt
3/4 cup pear baby food
2 egg whites
2 teaspoons vanilla

Preheat oven to 375 degrees.

Combine oats, flour, sugar, cranberries, raisins, dates, cinnamon, cloves, baking soda, baking powder, and salt in a large mixing bowl.

Combine pears, egg whites, and vanilla in a small bowl and blend well. Add pear mixture to dry ingredients and mix with a fork until blended. Drop by the tablespoonful onto a baking sheet that has been coated with vegetable spray. Bake for 12 minutes, or until cookies are golden. When cookies are cool, store in an airtight container.

Nutritional analysis per cookie:

79	Calories	7 %	Calories from Fat
2 g	Protein	2 g	Fiber
18 g	Carbohydrates	40 mg	Sodium
1 g	Fat	0 mg	Cholesterol

Cocoa Brownies

One can never have too many recipes for brownies! These rich and fudgy brownies are delicious with a cold glass of milk or a dish of nonfat frozen yogurt.

24 brownies

1/2 cup *each* unbleached flour, cocoa, and sugar
1/8 teaspoon salt
1/2 cup apricot butter (see Helpful Hints)
6 tablespoons light corn syrup
1/4 cup egg substitute
2 egg whites
1 1/2 teaspoons vanilla

Preheat oven to 350 degrees.

Combine flour, cocoa, sugar, and salt in a large mixing bowl.

Combine apricot butter, corn syrup, egg substitute, egg whites, and vanilla in a small bowl and blend well. Add apricot mixture to dry ingredients and mix with a fork until blended. Spoon batter into an 8-inch square baking pan that has been coated with vegetable spray and bake for 30 minutes, or until cake tester inserted into center of brownies comes out clean. Cool brownies in pan on a cake rack before cutting into squares.

Nutritional analysis per brownie:

51	Calories	7 %	Calories from Fat
1 g	Protein	1 g	Fiber
12 g	Carbohydrates	38 mg	Sodium
0 g	Fat	0 mg	Cholesterol

Cream Cheese Brownies

These epicurean brownies consist of a layer of cream cheese filling sandwiched between two layers of rich, chocolate brownie. They can be placed in attractive cupcake holders and served on a dessert buffet table or enjoyed as a petite lowfat indulgence.

16 brownies

1 bar (4 ounces) German's sweet chocolate
4 ounces light cream cheese, at room temperature
1/4 cup sugar
1 egg white
1 tablespoon unbleached flour
1/2 teaspoon vanilla
1/2 cup unbleached flour
3/4 cup sugar
1/2 teaspoon baking powder
1/4 teaspoon salt
5 tablespoons prune lekvar
1/2 cup egg substitute
1 teaspoon vanilla
1/4 teaspoon almond extract

Preheat oven to 350 degrees.

Place chocolate in a small heavy saucepan and cook, covered, over low heat, just until chocolate is soft enough to blend. Set aside.

Place cream cheese in work bowl of food processor and process until smooth. Add 1/4 cup sugar, egg white, 1 tablespoon flour, and 1/2 teaspoon vanilla; process until smooth. Set aside.

Combine 1/2 cup flour, 3/4 cup sugar, baking powder, and salt in a large mixing bowl.

Combine lekvar, egg substitute, 1 teaspoon vanilla, almond flavoring, and melted chocolate in a small bowl and blend well. Add chocolate mixture to dry ingredients and mix with a fork until blended. Set aside one cup of the chocolate batter.

Spread remaining chocolate batter in an 8-inch square baking pan that has been coated with vegetable spray. Spread cream cheese batter over chocolate batter. Randomly drop reserved chocolate batter by the tablespoonful over cream cheese batter. Swirl a knife through the batter to create a marble pattern. Bake for 35 to 45 minutes, or until cake tester inserted into center of brownies comes out clean. Cover brownies with waxed paper and cool on a cake rack. Cut into squares when cool and store in an airtight container.

Nutritional analysis per brownie:

136	Calories	26 %	Calories from Fat
2 g	Protein	1 g	Fiber
23 g	Carbohydrates	72 mg	Sodium
4 g	Fat	5 mg	Cholesterol

Date and Wheat Germ Bars

These exceptionally tasty bars can be made with any kind or a combination of dried fruit.

16 bars

1 cup toasted wheat germ
1/4 cup unbleached flour
3/4 cup sugar
1/2 cup powdered nonfat milk
1/2 teaspoon baking powder
1/8 teaspoon salt
1/2 cup chopped dates
1/4 cup pear baby food
2 egg whites
1 tablespoon molasses
1 tablespoon vanilla

Preheat oven to 350 degrees.

Combine wheat germ, flour, sugar, milk, baking powder, salt, and dates in a large mixing bowl.

Combine pears, egg whites, molasses, and vanilla in a small bowl and blend well. Add pear mixture to dry ingredients and mix with a fork until blended. Spoon batter into an 8-inch square baking pan that has been coated with vegetable spray. Bake for 30 minutes. Cut cookies into bars while still warm and store in an airtight container.

Nutritional analysis per bar:

101	Calories	9 %	Calories from Fat
3 g	Protein	1 g	Fiber
20 g	Carbohydrates	52 mg	Sodium
1 g	Fat	0 mg	Cholesterol

Festive Fruitcake Bonbons

Christmas is the perfect time of year to make these fruitcake bonbons.
They look beautiful on a holiday buffet table or make an attractive
gift when placed in a box lined with Christmas foil and tied with a red
ribbon.

24 bonbons

1/4 cup (2 ounces) frozen orange juice, thawed
Scant 1/3 cup molasses
1 cup raisins
2/3 cup mixed candied fruit (reserve 24 small pieces)
1/2 cup unbleached flour
1/4 cup sugar
1/4 cup chopped walnuts
1/2 teaspoon cinnamon
1/4 teaspon nutmeg
1/8 teaspoon *each* allspice and ground cloves
1/8 teaspoon baking soda
1/3 cup prune lekvar
1 egg white
2 tablespoons brandy

Preheat oven to 350 degrees.

Combine orange juice, molasses, and raisins in a small saucepan
over medium heat. Cook mixture until it comes to a boil, stirring
occasionally. Lower heat and simmer for 5 minutes. Remove from
heat and add candied fruit minus reserved pieces; blend well. Set
aside.

Combine flour, sugar, walnuts, cinnamon, nutmeg, allspice,
cloves, and baking soda in a large mixing bowl.

Combine lekvar and egg white in a small bowl. Add lekvar and
fruit mixture to dry ingredients and mix with a fork until blended.
Spoon mixture two-thirds full into paper-lined miniature muffin

tins and top each one with a piece of reserved candied fruit. Bake for 20 to 25 minutes. Cool bonbons on a cake rack. When cool, prick tops of bonbons with a fork and sprinkle each with 1/4 teaspoon brandy. Store in an airtight container.

Note: This recipe can be doubled or tripled easily.

Nutritional analysis per bonbon:

90	Calories	9 %	Calories from Fat
1 g	Protein	1 g	Fiber
20 g	Carbohydrates	12 mg	Sodium
1 g	Fat	0 mg	Cholesterol

Fruity Oatmeal Bars

A friend was given a recipe for fruity oatmeal bars that were made with butter and whole eggs. Since she was watching her fat intake, she asked me to try the recipe using puréed fruit and egg whites. The result was a very moist, fruity cookie that tasted delicious. Additional spices such as nutmeg, allspice, or ground cloves can be added to make a spicier bar.

24 bars

3 cups rolled oats
1 cup unbleached flour
1 cup firmly packed brown sugar
1 1/2 teaspoons cinnamon
1/2 teaspoon baking soda
2 jars (6 ounces each) pear baby food
2 egg whites
1 teaspoon vanilla
1 cup apple butter
1 heaping cup minced raisins, dates, apricots, or prunes (or any
      combination of dried fruits)

Preheat oven to 350 degrees.

Combine oats, flour, brown sugar, cinnamon, and baking soda in a large mixing bowl.

   Combine pears, egg whites, and vanilla in a small bowl and blend well. Add pear mixture to dry ingredients and mix with a fork until blended. Spread half of the batter onto the bottom of a 9-inch square baking pan that has been coated with vegetable spray. Spread apple butter over batter and sprinkle with dried fruits. Spoon remaining batter over fruit and spread carefully to completely cover. Bake for 35 minutes. Cut into bars while slightly warm.

Nutritional analysis per bar:

169	Calories	5 %	Calories from Fat
3 g	Protein	3 g	Fiber
39 g	Carbohydrates	30 mg	Sodium
1 g	Fat	0 mg	Cholesterol

Harvest-Time Pumpkin Cookies

These chunky cookies can be made with raisins instead of chocolate chips. Either way, they are a tasty treat and make a great snack at any time of the day.

18 cookies

2 cups unbleached flour
1 cup sugar
2 teaspoons baking powder
1 teaspoon baking soda
1 teaspoon cinnamon
1/4 teaspoon salt
1 cup chocolate chips or raisins
1 cup solid-pack canned pumpkin
1/2 cup prune lekvar
1 egg white
2 teaspoons vanilla

Preheat oven to 375 degrees.

Combine flour, sugar, baking powder, baking soda, cinnamon, salt, and chocolate chips in a large mixing bowl.

Combine pumpkin, lekvar, egg white, and vanilla in a small bowl and blend well. Add pumpkin mixture to dry ingredients and mix with a fork until blended. Drop dough by the teaspoonful onto a baking sheet that has been coated with vegetable spray. Bake for 11 to 12 minutes, or until cookies are golden brown.

Nutritional analysis per cookie:

Cookie with chocolate chips:

168	Calories	19 %	Calories from Fat
2 g	Protein	1 g	Fiber
33 g	Carbohydrates	122 mg	Sodium
4 g	Fat	0 mg	Cholesterol

Cookie with raisins:

148	Calories	1 %	Calories from Fat
2 g	Protein	2 g	Fiber
35 g	Carbohydrates	121 mg	Sodium
0 g	Fat	0 mg	Cholesterol

Hearty Fruit and Nut Bars

This is an adaption of the Energy Bars recipe from a cookbook I wrote with Jo Gail Wenzel and Ellie Densen The Prune Gourmet.

24 bars

1 cup *each* unbleached flour, whole wheat flour, and
    quick-cooking oats
1 cup firmly packed light brown sugar
1/2 cup toasted wheat germ
3/4 cup *each* whole almonds and chocolate chips
1/2 cup *each* chopped dates and apricots
1/2 cup prune lekvar
4 egg whites
1 tablespoon canola oil
1 teaspoon vanilla

Preheat oven to 350 degrees.

Combine flours, oats, brown sugar, wheat germ, almonds, chocolate chips, dates, and apricots in a large mixing bowl.

Combine lekvar, egg whites, oil, and vanilla in a small bowl and blend well. Add lekvar mixture to dry ingredients and mix with a fork until blended. Press batter into a 9 × 13-inch baking pan that has been coated with vegetable spray and bake for 35 minutes. Cool before cutting into squares.

Nutritional analysis per bar:

171	Calories	27 %	Calories from Fat
4 g	Protein	3 g	Fiber
29 g	Carbohydrates	33 mg	Sodium
5 g	Fat	0 mg	Cholesterol

Linzer Cookies

Almonds, spices, and raspberries create a symphony of flavors in these irresistible cookies. Serve them with sorbet after a rich meal or enjoy as an indulgence during an afternoon coffee break.

24 cookies

1 1/2 cups unbleached flour
1/2 cup firmly packed dark brown sugar
1/4 cup granulated sugar
1/2 cup almonds, finely ground
1/2 teaspoon baking powder
1/8 teaspoon salt
1 teaspoon cinnamon
1/8 teaspoon *each* ground cloves and allspice
1/2 cup prune lekvar
2 egg whites
1/2 cup raspberry jam

Preheat oven to 375 degrees.

Combine flour, sugars, almonds, baking powder, salt, cinnamon, cloves, and allspice in a large mixing bowl.

Combine lekvar and egg whites in a small bowl and blend well. Add lekvar mixture to dry ingredients and mix with a fork until blended. Press two-thirds of the batter evenly onto the bottom of a 9-inch square baking pan that has been coated with vegetable spray. Spread raspberry jam over dough leaving a 1/4-inch border on all sides. Drop remaining batter by the teaspoonful randomly over jam. Bake for 30 minutes. Cut into bars when cool and store in an airtight container.

Nutritional analysis per cookie:

103	Calories	13 %	Calories from Fat
2 g	Protein	1 g	Fiber
21 g	Carbohydrates	27 mg	Sodium
2 g	Fat	0 mg	Cholesterol

Lowfat Chocolate Chip Cookies

This recipe appears courtesy of the California Prune Board.

60 cookies

1 cup prune lekvar or prune butter (see Helpful Hints)
3 large egg whites
1 teaspoon vanilla
3/4 cup granulated sugar
3/4 cup firmly packed dark brown sugar
2 1/4 cups unbleached flour
1 teaspoon baking soda
1 teaspoon salt
2 cups (12 ounces) chocolate chips

Preheat oven to 375 degrees.

Combine lekvar, egg whites, and vanilla in a small bowl and blend well.

Combine sugars, flour, baking soda, salt, and chocolate chips in a large mixing bowl. Add lekvar mixture to dry ingredients and mix with a fork until blended. Drop by the tablespoonful onto baking sheets that have been coated with vegetable spray and flatten slightly. Bake cookies for about 10 minutes until lightly browned around edges. Remove to racks to cool completely.

Nutritional analysis per cookie:

74	Calories	24 %	Calories from Fat
1 g	Protein	0 g	Fiber
14 g	Carbohydrates	55 mg	Sodium
2 g	Fat	0 mg	Cholesterol

Lowfat Fudgy Brownies

This recipe appears courtesy of the California Prune Board.

36 brownies

4 ounces unsweetened chocolate
1/2 cup prune lekvar or prune butter (see Helpful Hints)
3 egg whites
1 teaspoon vanilla
1 cup sugar
1 teaspoon salt
1/2 cup unbleached flour
1/4 cup chopped walnuts

Preheat oven to 350 degrees.

Cut chocolate into 1-inch pieces and place in heat-proof bowl. Set over low heat in small skillet containing 1/2-inch simmering water. Stir occasionally just until chocolate is melted. Remove from heat; set aside.

Combine lekvar, egg whites, and vanilla in a small bowl and blend well.

Combine sugar, salt, and flour in a large mixing bowl. Add prune mixture and melted chocolate to dry ingredients and mix with a fork until blended. Spoon batter into an 8-inch square baking pan that has been coated with vegetable spray; sprinkle with walnuts. Bake for about 30 minutes, or until springy to the touch about 2 inches around edges. Cool on rack. Cut into 1 1/2-inch squares.

Nutritional analysis per brownie:

57	Calories	25 %	Calories from Fat
1 g	Protein	0 g	Fiber
10 g	Carbohydrates	65 mg	Sodium
2 g	Fat	0 mg	Cholesterol

Cookies and Bars

Milk Chocolate Brownies

The hardest part about making these brownies is not eating the choco-late chips before they're added to the batter!

16 brownies

2/3 cup unbleached flour
1 cup sugar
1/2 cup Dutch process cocoa
1/2 teaspoon baking powder
1/2 cup milk chocolate chips
1/2 cup prune lekvar
3 egg whites
1 teaspoon vanilla

Preheat oven to 350 degrees.

Combine flour, sugar, cocoa, baking powder, and milk chocolate chips in a large mixing bowl.

Combine lekvar, egg whites, and vanilla in a small bowl and blend well. Add lekvar mixture to dry ingredients and mix with a fork until blended. Spoon batter into an 8-inch square baking pan that has been coated with vegetable spray. Bake for 30 to 35 minutes, or until cake tester inserted into center of cake comes out clean. Cover with waxed paper and cool on a cake rack. When brownies are cool, cut into squares and store in an airtight container.

Nutritional analysis per brownie:

119	Calories	15 %	Calories from Fat
1 g	Protein	1 g	Fiber
25 g	Carbohydrates	26 mg	Sodium
2 g	Fat	0 mg	Cholesterol

Oatmeal and Peanut Butter Cookies

*These chunky cookies are overflowing with good things to eat . . .
raisins, chocolate chips, oats, and peanut butter. They make a great
snack to be enjoyed at any time of the day or as a super treat to add to
the lunch box.*

24 cookies

1 cup unbleached flour
1/2 cup *each* granulated sugar and firmly packed
     dark brown sugar
1/2 teaspoon *each* baking soda and salt
1 cup rolled oats
1 cup chocolate chips or raisins
6 tablespoons pear baby food
6 tablespoons chunky peanut butter
1 egg white
2 tablespoons skim milk
1 teaspoon vanilla

Preheat oven to 350 degrees.

Combine flour, sugars, baking soda, salt, oats, and chocolate chips
in a large mixing bowl.

    Combine pears, peanut butter, egg white, milk, and vanilla in a
small bowl and mix well. Add pear mixture to dry ingredients and
mix with a fork until blended. Drop by the tablespoonful, 2 inches
apart, onto a baking sheet that has been coated with vegetable
spray. Bake for 14 to 16 minutes, or until cookies are golden
brown. Cool. Store cookies in an airtight container. These cookies
taste best when allowed to sit for 24 hours.

Nutritional analysis per cookie:

Cookie with chocolate chips:

129	Calories	32 %	Calories from Fat
3 g	Protein	1 g	Fiber
20 g	Carbohydrates	87 mg	Sodium
5 g	Fat	0 mg	Cholesterol

Cookie with raisins:

113	Calories	18 %	Calories from Fat
3 g	Protein	1 g	Fiber
22 g	Carbohydrates	86 mg	Sodium
2 g	Fat	0 mg	Cholesterol

Oatmeal Cookies

This recipe appears courtesy of the California Prune Board.

30 cookies

1/2 cup *each* granulated sugar and brown sugar
1 tablespoon nonfat milk
1 cup unbleached flour
1/2 teaspoon *each* baking soda, baking powder, and salt
1 cup rolled oats
1/4 cup prune purée (recipe follows)
1/4 cup water
1 teaspoon vanilla

Preheat oven to 350 degrees.

Combine sugars, milk, flour, baking soda, baking powder, salt, and oats in a large mixing bowl.

Combine prune purée, water, and vanilla in a small bowl and blend well. Add prune mixture to dry ingredients and mix with a fork until blended. Drop by the generous teaspoonful, spaced apart, onto baking sheets that have been coated with vegetable spray. Bake for 12 minutes. Remove to racks to cool completely. Store in an airtight container up to 2 weeks.

To make prune purée: Combine 1/3 cup (2 ounces) pitted prunes and 1 1/2 tablespoons water in container of food processor. Pulse on and off until prunes are finely chopped. Makes 1/4 cup.

Nutritional analysis per cookie:

59	Calories	3 %	Calories from Fat
1 g	Protein	1 g	Fiber
13 g	Carbohydrates	58 mg	Sodium
0 g	Fat	0 mg	Cholesterol

Oatmeal, Raisin, and Millet Cookies

Millet is a cereal grain commonly used to make porridge, gruel, or flatbread. It complements the oatmeal and raisins in these simple cookies.

28 cookies

1 cup rolled oats
2/3 cup unbleached flour
1/3 cup whole wheat flour
1/3 cup *each* granulated sugar and firmly packed dark
  brown sugar
1/2 teaspoon baking soda
1/8 teaspoon salt
1/2 cup raisins
3 tablespoons millet
1 jar (6 ounces) pear baby food
1 egg white
2 teaspoons vanilla

Preheat oven to 350 degrees.

Combine oats, flours, sugars, baking soda, salt, raisins, and millet in a large mixing bowl.

Combine pears, egg white, and vanilla in a small bowl; blend well. Add pear mixture to dry ingredients and mix with a fork until blended. Drop by the tablespoonful, 2 inches apart, onto a baking sheet that has been coated with vegetable spray. Bake for 9 to 11 minutes, or until cookies are golden. Cool cookies for a couple of minutes before removing from baking sheet to cool completely.

Nutritional analysis per cookie:

55	Calories	4 %	Calories from Fat
1 g	Protein	1 g	Fiber
12 g	Carbohydrates	41 mg	Sodium
0 g	Fat	0 mg	Cholesterol

Paul Bunyan Cookies

These jumbo cookies are an all-time favorite. They are chewy, rich, and bursting with tasty ingredients. Raisins or chopped dates can be added for extra nutrition and texture.

24 cookies

1 1/2 cups rolled oats
1 1/2 cups unbleached flour
1/2 teaspoon baking soda
1/4 teaspoon salt
1 cup *each* granulated sugar and firmly packed dark
  brown sugar
1 cup chocolate chips
1 jar (6 ounces) pear baby food
1/2 cup crunchy peanut butter
2 egg whites
1 teaspoon vanilla

Preheat oven to 350 degrees.

Combine oats, flour, baking soda, salt, sugars, and chocolate chips in a large mixing bowl.

Combine pears, peanut butter, egg whites, and vanilla in a small bowl and blend well. Add peanut butter mixture to dry ingredients and mix with a fork until blended. Using an ice-cream scoop, spoon dough 4 inches apart onto a baking sheet that has been coated with vegetable spray and bake for 15 minutes, or until cookies are golden.

Nutritional analysis per cookie:

188	Calories	26 %	Calories from Fat
4 g	Protein	1 g	Fiber
33 g	Carbohydrates	74 mg	Sodium
6 g	Fat	0 mg	Cholesterol

Peanut Butter and Chocolate Chip Bars

Peanut butter was created in 1890 by a physician who was concerned about his elderly patients who were toothless and unable to chew food. Because peanuts are high in protein and easily digested, he thought his creation would be an excellent way to provide protein in their diets. These peanut butter cookies studded with chocolate chips are the ultimate treat.

48 bars

1 cup unbleached flour
3/4 cup chocolate chips
3/4 cup sugar
1/8 teaspoon salt
1/2 cup peanut butter
6 tablespoons pear baby food
3 egg whites
1 teaspoon vanilla

Preheat oven to 350 degrees.

Combine flour, chocolate chips, sugar, and salt in a large mixing bowl.

Combine peanut butter, pears, egg whites, and vanilla in work bowl of food processor and process until smooth. Add peanut butter mixture to dry ingredients and mix with a fork until blended. Spread batter into a 9-inch square baking pan that has been coated with vegetable spray and bake for 30 to 35 minutes, or until edges are lightly browned. Cut into squares while slightly warm.

Note: Try making these cookies with the new reduced-fat peanut butters that are now available.

Nutritional analysis per bar:

52	Calories	38 %	Calories from Fat
1 g	Protein	1 g	Fiber
7 g	Carbohydrates	22 mg	Sodium
2 g	Fat	0 mg	Cholesterol

Peanut Butter Cookies

Children will love these cookies. For an added treat, top each cookie with a chocolate kiss as soon as they come out of the oven.

36 cookies

1 cup unbleached flour
1/2 cup *each* granulated sugar and brown sugar
1/2 teaspoon baking soda
1/4 teaspoon salt
1 jar (6 ounces) pear baby food
1/2 cup peanut butter
1 egg white
1/2 teaspoon vanilla

Preheat oven to 350 degrees.

Combine flour, sugars, baking soda, and salt in a large mixing bowl.

Combine pears, peanut butter, egg white, and vanilla in a small bowl and blend well. Add peanut butter mixture to dry ingredients and mix with a fork until blended. Spoon dough by the teaspoonful onto a baking sheet that has been coated with vegetable spray. Bake for 14 to 16 minutes, or until cookies are golden brown.

Note: Try making these cookies with the new reduced-fat peanut butters that are now available.

Nutritional analysis per cookie:

48	Calories	34 %	Calories from Fat
1 g	Protein	0 g	Fiber
7 g	Carbohydrates	55 mg	Sodium
2 g	Fat	0 mg	Cholesterol

Salted Peanut and Chocolate Chip Cookies

These soft cookies are made with an irresistible combination of salted peanuts, chocolate chips, and peanut butter.

30 cookies

1 1/4 cups unbleached flour
1/2 cup firmly packed dark brown sugar
1/4 cup granulated sugar
1 teaspoon baking soda
1/4 teaspoon salt
1/2 cup *each* chocolate chips and Spanish peanuts
1 jar (6 ounces) pear baby food
1/4 cup peanut butter
1 egg white

Preheat oven to 325 degrees.

Combine flour, sugars, baking soda, salt, chocolate chips, and peanuts in a large mixing bowl.

Combine pears, peanut butter, and egg white in a small bowl and blend well. Add pear mixture to dry ingredients and mix with a fork until blended. Drop by the tablespoonful, 1 inch apart, onto a baking sheet that has been coated with vegetable spray. Bake for 15 minutes, or until cookies are golden brown.

Note: Try making these cookies with the new reduced-fat peanut butters that are now available.

Nutritional analysis per cookie:

82	Calories	35 %	Calories from Fat
2 g	Protein	1 g	Fiber
12 g	Carbohydrates	60 mg	Sodium
3 g	Fat	0 mg	Cholesterol

Solo Lowfat Brownies

This recipe for lowfat cakelike brownies is featured on the label of cans of Solo brand Prune Plum (Lekvar) Filling.

24 brownies

3/4 cup prune-plum lekvar
1 1/4 cups water
4 egg whites
2 teaspoons vanilla
1 1/2 cups unbleached flour
1 1/2 cups sugar
1 cup cocoa
2 teaspoons baking powder
1/2 teaspoon baking soda
1/2 teaspoon salt
1/2 cup chopped walnuts (optional)

Preheat oven to 350 degrees.

Place lekvar, water, egg whites, and vanilla in a large bowl and mix well.

In separate bowl, stir together flour, sugar, cocoa, baking powder, baking soda, and salt. Add filling mixture and mix thoroughly. Spread batter evenly in a 9 × 13-inch baking pan that has been coated with vegetable spray. Sprinkle walnuts on top. Bake 20 to 25 minutes. Cool and cut into squares.

Nutritional analysis per brownie:

Brownie without walnuts:

111	Calories	6 %	Calories from Fat
2 g	Protein	2 g	Fiber
25 g	Carbohydrates	129 mg	Sodium
1 g	Fat	0 mg	Cholesterol

Brownie with walnuts:

127	Calories	16 %	Calories from Fat
2 g	Protein	2 g	Fiber
26 g	Carbohydrates	130 mg	Sodium
2 g	Fat	0 mg	Cholesterol

Spicy Chews

16 cookies

2 1/4 cups unbleached flour
1 cup firmly packed dark brown sugar
1 teaspoon baking soda
1 teaspoon *each* cinnamon and ginger
1/2 teaspoon ground cloves
1/4 teaspoon salt
3/4 cup prune lekvar
2 tablespoons molasses
1 egg white

Preheat oven to 375 degrees.

Combine flour, brown sugar, baking soda, cinnamon, ginger, cloves, and salt in a large mixing bowl.

Combine lekvar, molasses, and egg white in work bowl of food processor; process until smooth. Add lekvar mixture to dry ingredients and mix with a fork until blended. Drop dough by the teaspoonful onto a cookie sheet that has been coated with vegetable spray. Spray bottom of fork with vegetable spray and flatten cookies. Bake for 10 minutes, or until cookies are firm but not hard. Cool completely. Store cookies in an airtight container.

Nutritional analysis per cookie:

153	Calories	1 %	Calories from Fat
2 g	Protein	1 g	Fiber
36 g	Carbohydrates	101 mg	Sodium
0 g	Fat	0 mg	Cholesterol

Spicy Oatmeal Cookies

These old-fashioned cookies are crisp, spicy, and good to the last bite.

36 cookies

2 cups rolled oats
1 3/4 cups unbleached flour
1 cup sugar
1 teaspoon baking soda
1 teaspoon cinnamon
1/4 teaspoon salt
1/2 cup raisins
1/2 cup prune lekvar
2 egg whites
1/3 cup molasses

Preheat oven to 350 degrees.

Combine oats, flour, sugar, baking soda, cinnamon, salt, and raisins in a large mixing bowl.

Combine lekvar, egg whites, and molasses in a small bowl and blend well. Add lekvar mixture to dry ingredients and mix with a fork until blended. Drop dough by the tablespoonful onto a baking sheet that has been coated with vegetable spray. Bake for 15 to 16 minutes, or until cookies are firm to the touch.

Nutritional analysis per cookie:

77	Calories	4 %	Calories from Fat
2 g	Protein	1 g	Fiber
17 g	Carbohydrates	42 mg	Sodium
0 g	Fat	0 mg	Cholesterol

Spicy Oatmeal, Peanut Butter, and Raisin Cookies

These moist and chunky cookies are a favorite with my children and their friends.

24 cookies

2 cups unbleached flour
1 1/2 cups quick-cooking oats
1 cup *each* granulated sugar and firmly packed
    light brown sugar
1 teaspoon *each* baking soda and cinnamon
1/2 teaspoon salt
1 cup raisins
1 jar (6 ounces) pear baby food
1/2 cup peanut butter
2 egg whites
1/4 cup skim milk
1 teaspoon vanilla

Preheat oven to 350 degrees.

Combine flour, oats, sugars, baking soda, cinnamon, salt, and raisins in a large mixing bowl.

Combine pears, peanut butter, egg whites, milk, and vanilla in a small bowl and blend well. Add pear mixture to dry ingredients and mix with a fork until blended. Drop by the heaping tablespoonful, 1 inch apart, onto a baking sheet that has been coated with vegetable spray. Bake for 15 to 18 minutes, or until cookies are golden brown.

Note: Try making these cookies with the new reduced-fat peanut butters that are now available.

Nutritional analysis per cookie:

173	Calories	15 %	Calories from Fat
3 g	Protein	1 g	Fiber
34 g	Carbohydrates	138 mg	Sodium
3 g	Fat	0 mg	Cholesterol

Tangy Lemon and Orange Bars

16 bars

2 1/4 cups unbleached flour
1 cup sugar
1 tablespoon baking powder
1/8 teaspoon salt
1 teaspoon *each* finely grated lemon peel and orange peel
1 jar (6 ounces) pear baby food
1/4 cup *each* fresh lemon juice and orange juice
3 egg whites

Preheat oven to 350 degrees.

Combine flour, sugar, baking powder, salt, lemon peel, and orange peel in a large mixing bowl.

Combine pears, juices, and egg whites in a small bowl and mix well. Add juice mixture to dry ingredients and mix with a fork until blended. Pour batter into an 8 × 11.5 × 2-inch oblong baking dish that has been coated with vegetable spray and bake for 30 to 35 minutes, or until cake tester inserted into center of cake comes out clean. Cover cake with waxed paper and cool on a cake rack. Cut into bars while slightly warm and store in an airtight container.

Nutritional analysis per bar:

118	Calories	3 %	Calories from Fat
3 g	Protein	2 g	Fiber
27 g	Carbohydrates	89 mg	Sodium
0 g	Fat	0 mg	Cholesterol

Trick-or-Treat Pumpkin Bars

Halloween is my favorite time of year to make these pumpkin bars for my children and their friends. They are delicately spiced and very rich in flavor.

18 bars

Pumpkin Cake
2 cups unbleached flour
1 1/2 cups granulated sugar
2 teaspoons *each* baking powder and cinnamon
1 teaspoon baking soda
1/8 teaspoon salt
1 can (16 ounces) solid-pack pumpkin
1 jar (6 ounces) pear baby food
2 tablespoons canola oil
4 egg whites

Cream Cheese Frosting
6 ounces light cream cheese, at room temperature
1 cup powdered sugar
1 teaspoon vanilla

Preheat oven to 350 degrees.

To make pumpkin cake: Combine flour, sugar, baking powder, cinnamon, baking soda, and salt in a large mixing bowl.

Combine pumpkin, pears, oil, and egg whites in a small bowl and blend well. Add pumpkin mixture to dry ingredients and mix with a fork until blended. Spoon batter into a 9 × 13-inch baking pan that has been coated with vegetable spray. Bake for 25 to 30 minutes, or until cake tester inserted into center of cake comes out clean. Cover cake with waxed paper and cool on a cake rack.

To make cream cheese frosting: Place cream cheese in mixing bowl of electric mixer and beat just until smooth. Add sugar and vanilla; beat until smooth. Spread on cooled pumpkin cake.

Refrigerate pumpkin cake, covered, for several hours. Cut into bars before serving.

Nutritional analysis per bar:

Cake:

154	Calories	12 %	Calories from Fat
3 g	Protein	1 g	Fiber
31 g	Carbohydrates	111 mg	Sodium
2 g	Fat	0 mg	Cholesterol

Frosting:

46	Calories	39 %	Calories from Fat
1 g	Protein	0 g	Fiber
6 g	Carbohydrates	38 mg	Sodium
2 g	Fat	7 mg	Cholesterol

Total:

200	Calories	18 %	Calories from Fat
4 g	Protein	1 g	Fiber
37 g	Carbohydrates	148 mg	Sodium
4 g	Fat	7 mg	Cholesterol

Wholesome Oatmeal Cookies

These exceptionally moist cookies are chock-full of good things to eat. . . . It's hard to eat just one!

42 cookies

3/4 cup whole wheat flour
3/4 cup firmly packed dark brown sugar
1/2 cup rolled oats
1/4 cup toasted wheat germ
3/4 cup raisins
1/4 cup *each* sunflower seeds and sesame seeds
1/2 teaspoon baking powder
1/4 teaspoon salt
1 1/2 teaspoons cinnamon
1/4 teaspoon *each* ground cloves and allspice
1/8 teaspoon ginger
1/2 cup apple butter
1/4 cup reduced-fat peanut butter
1/4 cup egg substitute
2 tablespoons skim milk

Preheat oven to 375 degrees.

Combine flour, brown sugar, oats, wheat germ, raisins, sunflower seeds, sesame seeds, baking powder, salt, cinnamon, cloves, allspice, and ginger in a large mixing bowl.

Combine apple butter, peanut butter, egg substitute, and milk in a small bowl and blend well. Add apple butter mixture to dry ingredients and mix with a fork until blended. Drop by the tablespoonful, 1 inch apart, onto a baking sheet that has been coated with vegetable spray. Bake for 18 minutes, or until cookies are firm to the touch.

Nutritional analysis per cookie:

70	Calories	26 %	Calories from Fat
2 g	Protein	1 g	Fiber
11 g	Carbohydrates	23 mg	Sodium
2 g	Fat	0 mg	Cholesterol

Zippy Zucchini Bars

These spicy zucchini bars are full of fruit and bran and are loaded with nutrition.

24 bars

1¹/2 cups unbleached flour
¹/2 cup whole wheat flour
1 cup 100% bran cereal
³/4 cup firmly packed dark brown sugar
1 teaspoon baking soda
¹/4 teaspoon salt
¹/2 teaspoon cinnamon
¹/4 teaspoon nutmeg
1 cup chopped mixed dried fruit
1 pound (2 ¹/2 cups) grated zucchini
1 jar (6 ounces) applesauce baby food
2 egg whites
1 teaspoon vanilla

Preheat oven to 350 degrees.

Combine flours, cereal, sugar, baking soda, salt, cinnamon, nutmeg, and fruit in a large mixing bowl.

Combine zucchini, applesauce, egg whites, and vanilla in a small bowl and blend well. Add zucchini mixture to dry ingredients and mix with a fork until blended. Spoon batter into a 9 × 13-inch baking pan that has been coated with vegetable spray and bake for 40 minutes, or until cake tester inserted into center of cake comes out clean. Cut into bars when cool.

Nutritional analysis per bar:

97	Calories	3 %	Calories from Fat
2 g	Protein	2 g	Fiber
23 g	Carbohydrates	84 mg	Sodium
0 g	Fat	0 mg	Cholesterol

Muffins

Apple and Date Muffins

These muffins taste delicious when enjoyed with a hot cup of coffee in the morning or when you need a lowfat but tasty quick snack in the afternoon.

12 muffins

1/2 cup chopped dried dates
1 cup apple juice
1 cup whole wheat flour
1 cup oat bran
1/4 cup rolled oats
1 teaspoon baking soda
1 tablespoon cinnamon
1/8 teaspoon *each* allspice, nutmeg, and ginger
1/2 cup plain nonfat yogurt
2 tablespoons honey
1 tablespoon molasses
1 egg white

Preheat oven to 400 degrees.

Combine dates and apple juice in a medium-size bowl and let sit for 10 minutes, or until dates are soft.

Combine flour, bran, oats, baking soda, cinnamon, allspice, nutmeg, and ginger in a large mixing bowl.

Add yogurt, honey, molasses, and egg white to apple juice and dates and blend well. Add apple juice mixture to dry ingredients and mix with a fork until just blended. Spoon batter just to the tops of muffin cups that have been coated with vegetable spray. Bake for 20 minutes, or until golden brown. Immediately remove muffins from pan. When muffins are cool, store in an airtight container. The muffins taste best when allowed to sit for 24 hours.

Nutritional analysis per muffin:

112	Calories	7 %	Calories from Fat
4 g	Protein	4 g	Fiber
26 g	Carbohydrates	83 mg	Sodium
1 g	Fat	0 mg	Cholesterol

Banana Crunch Muffins

These muffins are a variation of the Banana-Prune Crunchy Muffins featured in my cookbook The Prune Gourmet.

12 muffins

1 cup unbleached flour
2/3 cup whole wheat flour
1/4 cup toasted wheat germ
1 1/2 cups granola
1/4 cup firmly packed dark brown sugar
1 tablespoon baking powder
1/2 teaspoon baking soda
1/4 teaspoon salt
1/2 cup skim milk
1/2 cup pear baby food
2 medium-size ripe bananas, mashed
1 egg white

Preheat oven to 400 degrees.

Combine flours, wheat germ, granola, brown sugar, baking powder, baking soda, and salt in a large mixing bowl.

Combine milk, pears, bananas, and egg white in a small bowl and blend well. Add banana mixture to dry ingredients and mix with a fork until just blended. Spoon batter just to the tops of muffin cups that have been coated with vegetable spray. Bake for 18 minutes, or until tops are golden brown. Immediately remove muffins from pan. When muffins are cool, store in an airtight container. The muffins taste best when allowed to sit for 24 hours.

Nutritional analysis per muffin:

183	Calories	22 %	Calories from Fat
5 g	Protein	3 g	Fiber
32 g	Carbohydrates	165 mg	Sodium
5 g	Fat	0 mg	Cholesterol

Blueberry Muffins

A delicious lowfat snack as well as a wonderful addition to breakfast.

14 muffins

3 cups unbleached flour
1 cup sugar
1 tablespoon baking powder
1/2 teaspoon salt
1 cup skim milk
2/3 cup pear baby food
3 egg whites
1 1/3 cups fresh or frozen blueberries

Preheat oven to 375 degrees.

Combine flour, sugar, baking powder, and salt in a large mixing bowl.

Combine milk, pears, and egg whites in a small bowl and blend well. Add blueberries and stir to blend. Add blueberry mixture to dry ingredients and mix with a fork until just blended. Spoon batter just to the tops of muffin cups that have been coated with vegetable spray. Bake for 15 to 18 minutes, or until muffins are golden brown. Immediately remove muffins from pan. When muffins are cool, store in an airtight container. The muffins taste best when allowed to sit for 24 hours.

Variation: Substitute 6 ounces (1 cup) dried Bing cherries for the blueberries.

Nutritional analysis per muffin:

203	Calories	2 %	Calories from Fat
5 g	Protein	2 g	Fiber
46 g	Carbohydrates	160 mg	Sodium
0 g	Fat	0 mg	Cholesterol

Bran and Dried Fruit Muffins

This recipe was given to me by a friend who, when she made it the first time, realized too late in the baking that she had forgotten to include 1/4 cup of melted butter. We decided that the reason the muffins turned out so well anyway was the quantity of dried fruit included in the recipe. These delicious muffins are an excellent source of fiber.

12 muffins

1 1/2 cups original All-Bran cereal
1 1/4 cups skim milk
1 1/2 cups unbleached flour
1/2 cup sugar
1 teaspoon baking powder
1/4 teaspoon salt
1/2 cup *each* minced dried figs and dried apricots
1/4 cup *each* minced dried peaches and raisins
1 egg white
1/4 cup molasses
2 tablespoons prune baby food

Preheat oven to 400 degrees.

Combine cereal and milk in a medium-size bowl and set aside.

Combine flour, sugar, baking powder, salt, figs, apricots, peaches, and raisins in a large mixing bowl.

Add egg white, molasses, and prunes to cereal mixture and blend well. Add cereal mixture to dry ingredients and mix with a fork until just blended. Spoon batter just to the tops of muffin cups that have been coated with vegetable spray. Bake for 20 to 25 minutes, or until tops are golden brown. Immediately remove muffins from pan. When muffins are cool, store in an airtight container. The muffins taste best when allowed to sit for 24 hours.

Nutritional analysis per muffin:

198	Calories	2 %	Calories from Fat
5 g	Protein	6 g	Fiber
48 g	Carbohydrates	211 mg	Sodium
1 g	Fat	0 mg	Cholesterol

Coffee and Chocolate Chip Muffins

Coffee is the dominant flavor in these unusual muffins. Enjoy them during a coffee break or with an icy cold glass of skim milk.

12 muffins

1 3/4 cups unbleached flour
1/2 cup *each* granulated sugar and firmly packed dark
   brown sugar
1 tablespoon powdered instant coffee
1 tablespoon baking powder
1/4 teaspoon salt
1/2 cup chocolate chips
1/2 cup skim milk
1 jar (6 ounces) pear baby food
2 egg whites
1 tablespoon vanilla

Preheat oven to 400 degrees.

Combine flour, sugars, coffee, baking powder, salt, and chocolate chips in a large mixing bowl.

Combine milk, pears, egg whites, and vanilla in a small bowl. Add milk mixture to dry ingredients and mix with a fork until just blended. Spoon batter just to the tops of muffin cups that have been coated with vegetable spray. Bake for 20 minutes, or until golden brown. Immediately remove muffins from pan. When muffins are cool, store in an airtight container. The muffins taste best when allowed to sit for 24 hours.

Nutritional analysis per muffin:

189	Calories	14 %	Calories from Fat
3 g	Protein	1 g	Fiber
37 g	Carbohydrates	134 mg	Sodium
3 g	Fat	0 mg	Cholesterol

Cranberry Muffins

14 muffins

3 cups unbleached flour
1 cup sugar
1 tablespoon baking powder
1/4 teaspoon salt
1/2 teaspoon cinnamon
1 cup fresh or frozen cranberries, coarsely chopped
1 cup skim milk
1 jar (6 ounces) pear baby food
3 egg whites
1/2 teaspoon vanilla

Preheat oven to 375 degrees.

Combine flour, sugar, baking powder, salt, and cinnamon in a large mixing bowl.

Combine cranberries, milk, pears, egg whites, and vanilla in a small bowl and blend well. Add cranberry mixture to dry ingredients and mix with a fork until blended. Spoon batter just to the tops of muffin cups that have been coated with vegetable spray. Bake for 16 to 20 minutes, or until muffins are golden brown. Immediately remove muffins from pan. When muffins are cool, store in an airtight container. The muffins taste best when allowed to sit for 24 hours.

Nutritional analysis per muffin:

174	Calories	2 %	Calories from Fat
4 g	Protein	1 g	Fiber
38 g	Carbohydrates	122 mg	Sodium
0 g	Fat	0 mg	Cholesterol

Gingerbread Muffins

3 pts

I like to serve these spicy muffins at our Thanksgiving dinner. They complement the flavor of the turkey and the other traditional dishes served at this festive time of year.

8 muffins

1 cup unbleached flour
3/4 cup whole wheat flour
1/4 cup *each* firmly packed dark brown sugar and
    granulated sugar
1 teaspoon baking soda
1/4 teaspoon salt
1 teaspoon *each* ginger and cinnamon
1/4 teaspoon *each* allspice, nutmeg, and ground cloves
3/4 cup buttermilk
1/3 cup pear baby food
2 egg whites
1/4 cup molasses

Preheat oven to 400 degrees.

Combine flours, sugars, baking soda, salt, ginger, cinnamon, allspice, nutmeg, and cloves in a medium-size mixing bowl.

Combine buttermilk, pears, egg whites, and molasses in a small bowl and blend well. Add buttermilk mixture to dry ingredients and mix with a fork until just blended. Spoon batter just to the tops of muffin cups that have been coated with vegetable spray. Bake for 15 to 18 minutes, or until golden brown. Immediately remove muffins from pan. When muffins are cool, store in an airtight container. The muffins taste best when allowed to sit for 24 hours.

187	Calories	3 %	Calories from Fat
5 g	Protein	2 g	Fiber
41 g	Carbohydrates	212 mg	Sodium
1 g	Fat	1 mg	Cholesterol

Granny Smith Apple Muffins

The fusion of apples and spices in these autumnal muffins makes them a delicious accompaniment to hot apple cider or spiced tea.

12 muffins

2 cups unbleached flour
1/2 cup sugar
1 tablespoon baking powder
1/4 teaspoon salt
1 teaspoon cinnamon
1/4 teaspoon nutmeg
2 Granny Smith apples, peeled, cored, and chopped
1 cup skim milk
1/4 cup applesauce baby food
1 egg white

Preheat oven to 400 degrees.

Combine flour, sugar, baking powder, salt, cinnamon, and nutmeg in a large mixing bowl.

Combine apples, milk, applesauce, and egg white in a small bowl and blend well. Add apple mixture to dry ingredients and mix with a fork until just blended. Spoon batter just to the tops of muffin cups that have been coated with vegetable spray. Bake for 15 to 18 minutes, or until golden brown. Immediately remove muffins from pan. When muffins are cool, store in an airtight container. The muffins taste best when allowed to sit for 24 hours.

Nutritional analysis per muffin:

125	Calories	2 %	Calories from Fat
3 g	Protein	1 g	Fiber
27 g	Carbohydrates	133 mg	Sodium
0 g	Fat	0 mg	Cholesterol

Lemon Muffins   3 5 pts

These tart muffins are a nice accompaniment to a seafood or poultry dinner.

12 muffins

1 3/4 cups unbleached flour
3/4 cup sugar
1 teaspoon baking powder
3/4 teaspoon baking soda
1/4 teaspoon salt
1 container (8 ounces) lemon lowfat yogurt
1 jar (6 ounces) pear baby food
1 tablespoon fresh lemon juice
1 tablespoon finely grated lemon peel
1 egg white

Preheat oven to 400 degrees.

Combine flour, sugar, baking powder, baking soda, and salt in a large mixing bowl.

Combine yogurt, pears, lemon juice, lemon peel, and egg white in a small bowl and blend well. Add lemon mixture to dry ingredients and mix with a fork until just blended. Spoon batter just to the tops of muffin cups that have been coated with vegetable spray. Bake for 20 minutes, or until muffins are golden. Immediately remove muffins from pan. When muffins are cool, store in an airtight container. The muffins taste best when allowed to sit for 24 hours.

Nutritional analysis per muffin:

134	Calories	2 %	Calories from Fat
3 g	Protein	1 g	Fiber
30 g	Carbohydrates	137 mg	Sodium
0 g	Fat	0 mg	Cholesterol

Lowfat Bran-Apple Muffins

This recipe appears courtesy of the California Prune Board.

12 muffins

1 cup buttermilk
1 cup shredded bran cereal
1 teaspoon baking soda
1/2 cup firmly packed brown sugar
1/2 cup prune lekvar or prune butter (see Helpful Hints)
2 egg whites
1 tablespoon molasses
1 cup unbleached flour
1 cup peeled and grated apple (spooned, not packed into cup)
1/4 teaspoon salt

Preheat oven to 375 degrees.

Combine buttermilk, bran, and baking soda in a small bowl; set aside. In mixer bowl cream sugar and lekvar; beat in egg whites and molasses. Stir in buttermilk mixture, flour, apple, and salt and blend thoroughly. Spoon batter into muffin cups that have been coated with vegetable spray, dividing equally. Bake about 20 minutes, or until cake tester inserted into centers of muffins comes out clean. Cool in pan 15 minutes. Turn onto rack to cool completely.

Nutritional analysis per muffin:

116	Calories	4 %	Calories from Fat
3 g	Protein	2 g	Fiber
26 g	Carbohydrates	187 mg	Sodium
1 g	Fat	1 mg	Cholesterol

Morning Glory Muffins

Indulging in these high-fiber muffins, which are laden with fruits and vegetables, is a glorious way to start the morning.

16 muffins

1 1/2 cups unbleached flour
1/2 cup whole wheat flour
1 cup sugar
2 teaspoons cinnamon
2 teaspoons baking soda
1/4 teaspoon salt
1/2 cup raisins
1/2 pound carrots, cut into 2-inch chunks
1 Granny Smith apple, peeled, cored, and cut into wedges
1/2 cup prune lekvar
1/2 cup pear baby food
3 egg whites
1 teaspoon vanilla

Preheat oven to 350 degrees.

Combine flours, sugar, cinnamon, baking soda, salt, and raisins in a large mixing bowl.

In work bowl of food processor, process carrots and apple until chopped. Add prune lekvar, pears, egg whites, and vanilla and process until blended. Add carrot mixture to dry ingredients and mix with a fork until just blended. Spoon batter just to the tops of muffin cups that have been coated with vegetable spray. Bake for 40 to 45 minutes, or until golden brown. Immediately remove muffins from pan. When muffins are cool, store in an airtight container. The muffins taste best when allowed to sit for 24 hours.

Nutritional analysis per muffin:

157	Calories	2 %	Calories from Fat
3 g	Protein	2 g	Fiber
36 g	Carbohydrates	158 mg	Sodium
0 g	Fat	0 mg	Cholesterol

Oatmeal Muffins

These delicately spiced morsels are rich in fiber and flavor. They can be enjoyed at any time of the day.

12 muffins

1 cup rolled oats
3/4 cup oat bran
2/3 cup unbleached flour
1/4 cup firmly packed dark brown sugar
1 tablespoon baking powder
1/4 teaspoon salt
1 teaspoon *each* ground cloves and ginger
1/2 cup raisins
3/4 cup skim milk
1/4 cup molasses or honey
1/4 cup pear baby food
1 egg white

Preheat oven to 400 degrees.

Combine oats, bran, flour, brown sugar, baking powder, salt, cloves, ginger, and raisins in a large mixing bowl.

Combine milk, molasses, pears, and egg white in a small bowl and blend well. Add milk mixture to dry ingredients and mix with a fork until just blended. Spoon batter just to the tops of muffin cups that have been coated with vegetable spray. Bake for 15 to 18 minutes, or until golden. Immediately remove muffins from pan. When muffins are cool, store in an airtight container. The muffins taste best when allowed to sit for 24 hours.

Nutritional analysis per muffin:

128	Calories	7 %	Calories from Fat
4 g	Protein	2 g	Fiber
29 g	Carbohydrates	134 mg	Sodium
1 g	Fat	0 mg	Cholesterol

Orange Marmalade Muffins

This lowfat version of the Glazed Marmalade Muffins found in my cookbook The Prune Gourmet *combines the flavors of orange and prune with a tangy result.*

10 muffins

1 1/2 cups unbleached flour
1/2 cup sugar
2 teaspoons baking powder
1/2 teaspoon baking soda
1/4 teaspoon salt
1/2 teaspoon cinnamon
1/4 teapoon nutmeg
1 teaspoon finely grated orange peel
1/2 cup plain nonfat yogurt
1/3 cup prune baby food
1/4 cup orange marmalade
1 egg white

Preheat oven to 400 degrees.

Combine flour, sugar, baking powder, baking soda, salt, cinnamon, and nutmeg in a large mixing bowl.

Combine orange peel, yogurt, prunes, orange marmalade, and egg white in a small bowl. Add orange mixture to dry ingredients and mix with a fork until just blended. Spoon batter just to the tops of muffin cups that have been coated with vegetable spray. Bake for 20 minutes, or until golden brown. Immediately remove muffins from pan. When muffins are cool, store in an airtight container. The muffins taste best when allowed to sit for 24 hours.

Nutritional analysis per muffin:

145	Calories	1 %	Calories from Fat
3 g	Protein	1 g	Fiber
33 g	Carbohydrates	170 mg	Sodium
0 g	Fat	0 mg	Cholesterol

Peach Muffins

Not one but three different peach ingredients establish the unmistakable flavor of these moist muffins.

20 muffins

2 cups unbleached flour
1/2 cup sugar
2 teaspoons baking powder
1/2 teaspoon baking soda
1/4 teaspoon salt
1/2 teaspoon *each* cinnamon and nutmeg
1/2 cup minced dried peaches
1 container (8 ounces) peach lowfat yogurt
1/3 cup peach baby food
1/3 cup skim milk
1 egg white

Preheat oven to 400 degrees.

Combine flour, sugar, baking powder, baking soda, salt, cinnamon, nutmeg, and dried peaches in a large mixing bowl.

Combine yogurt, peach baby food, milk, and egg white in a small bowl and blend well. Add peach mixture to dry ingredients and mix with a fork until just blended. Spoon batter just to the tops of muffin cups that have been coated with vegetable spray. Bake for 20 minutes, or until golden. Immediately remove muffins from pan. When muffins are cool, store in an airtight container. The muffins taste best when allowed to sit for 24 hours.

Nutritional analysis per muffin:

95	Calories	3 %	Calories from Fat
2 g	Protein	1 g	Fiber
21 g	Carbohydrates	89 mg	Sodium
0 g	Fat	1 mg	Cholesterol

Peanut Butter Muffins

Spread a little jam on the tops of these muffins or eat them as they are; either way, you'll enjoy every bite.

8 muffins

1 1/2 cups unbleached flour
1/2 cup sugar
1 tablespoon baking powder
1/4 teaspoon salt
1 cup skim milk
1/2 cup creamy peanut butter
1/4 cup pear baby food
2 egg whites

Preheat oven to 400 degrees.

Combine flour, sugar, baking powder, and salt in a medium-size mixing bowl.

Combine milk, peanut butter, pears, and egg whites in a small bowl and blend well. Add peanut butter mixture to dry ingredients and mix with a fork until just blended. Spoon batter just to the tops of muffin cups that have been coated with vegetable spray. Bake for 25 minutes, or until golden. Immediately remove muffins from pan. When muffins are cool, store in an airtight container. The muffins taste best when allowed to sit for 24 hours.

Note: Try making these muffins with the new reduced-fat peanut butters that are now available.

Nutritional analysis per muffin:

249	Calories	29 %	Calories from Fat
8 g	Protein	2 g	Fiber
37 g	Carbohydrates	209 mg	Sodium
8 g	Fat	1 mg	Cholesterol

Pineapple Muffins

Crushed pineapple and pineapple juice add the perfect touch of sweetness to these delicious muffins.

20 muffins

1 can (20 ounces) unsweetened crushed pineapple
2/3 cup reserved pineapple juice
3 cups unbleached flour
1 cup sugar
1 tablespoon baking powder
1/4 teaspoon salt
1 cup skim milk
3 egg whites
1 teaspoon vanilla

Preheat oven to 400 degrees.

Place pineapple in a strainer over a bowl. Reserve 2/3 cup pineapple juice and the pineapple.

Combine flour, sugar, baking powder, and salt in a large mixing bowl.

Combine pineapple, reserved pineapple juice, milk, egg whites, and vanilla in a medium-size bowl and blend well. Add pineapple mixture to dry ingredients and mix with a fork until just blended. Spoon batter just to the tops of muffin cups that have been coated with vegetable spray. Bake for 20 minutes, or until golden. Immediately remove muffins from pan. When muffins are cool, store in an airtight container. The muffins taste best when allowed to sit for 24 hours.

Nutritional analysis per muffin:

139	Calories	1 %	Calories from Fat
3 g	Protein	1 g	Fiber
31 g	Carbohydrates	88 mg	Sodium
0 g	Fat	0 mg	Cholesterol

Poppy Seed Muffins

Poppy seeds add a slightly nutty flavor to these sweet muffins. Serve them at a morning coffee, brunch, or lunch.

12 muffins

2 cups unbleached flour
1 cup sugar
1 tablespoon baking powder
1/4 teaspoon baking soda
1/4 teaspoon salt
2 tablespoons poppy seeds
1 container (8 ounces) plain nonfat yogurt
1 jar (6 ounces) pear baby food
2 egg whites
1/2 tablespoon vanilla

Preheat oven to 400 degrees.

Combine flour, sugar, baking powder, baking soda, salt, and poppy seeds in a large mixing bowl.

Combine yogurt, pears, egg whites, and vanilla in a small bowl and blend well. Add yogurt mixture to dry ingredients and mix with a fork until just blended. Spoon batter just to the tops of muffin cups that have been coated with vegetable spray. Bake for 15 to 18 minutes, or until golden. Immediately remove muffins from pan. When muffins are cool, store in an airtight container. The muffins taste best when allowed to sit for 24 hours.

Nutritional analysis per muffin:

172	Calories	5 %	Calories from Fat
4 g	Protein	1 g	Fiber
36 g	Carbohydrates	159 mg	Sodium
1 g	Fat	0 mg	Cholesterol

Pumpkin Muffins

These light, spicy muffins will disappear fast. Serve them as a snack or as an accompaniment to a hearty stew.

8 muffins

3/4 cup unbleached flour
2/3 cup firmly packed brown sugar
1/4 teaspoon *each* baking powder and baking soda
1/8 teaspoon salt
1 teaspoon cinnamon
1/2 teaspoon ginger
1/4 teaspoon *each* ground cloves and nutmeg
1/8 teaspoon allspice
1/2 cup raisins
1/2 cup solid-pack canned pumpkin
1/2 cup pear baby food
1 egg white
1 1/2 teaspoons vanilla

Preheat oven to 400 degrees.

Combine flour, brown sugar, baking powder, baking soda, salt, cinnamon, ginger, cloves, nutmeg, allspice, and raisins in a large mixing bowl.

Combine pumpkin, pears, egg white, and vanilla in a small bowl and blend well. Add pumpkin mixture to dry ingredients and mix with a fork until just blended. Spoon batter just to the tops of muffin cups that have been coated with vegetable spray. Bake for 25 minutes, or until golden brown. Immediately remove muffins from pan. When muffins are cool, store in an airtight container. The muffins taste best when allowed to sit for 24 hours.

Nutritional analysis per muffin:

164	Calories	2 %	Calories from Fat
2 g	Protein	1 g	Fiber
38 g	Carbohydrates	84 mg	Sodium
0 g	Fat	0 mg	Cholesterol

Raspberry Muffins

Bring summertime to any meal by serving these wonderful muffins.
They can be a delicious accompaniment to a barbecued chicken dinner
or can add a special touch to a romantic Valentine's Day dinner.

10 muffins

1 1/2 cups unbleached flour
2 tablespoons whole wheat flour
1 cup sugar
1/2 teaspoon baking soda
1/4 teaspoon salt
2 teaspoons cinnamon
1 package (12 ounces) frozen unsweetened raspberries,
　　thawed and drained
2 egg whites
1 jar (6 ounces) pear baby food

Preheat oven to 400 degrees.

Combine flours, sugar, baking soda, salt, and cinnamon in a
medium-size mixing bowl.

Combine raspberries, egg whites, and pears in a small bowl
and blend well. Add raspberry mixture to dry ingredients and mix
with a fork until just blended. Spoon batter just to the tops of
muffin cups that have been coated with vegetable spray. Bake for
30 minutes, or until golden brown. Immediately remove muffins
from pan. When muffins are cool, store in an airtight container.
The muffins taste best when allowed to sit for 24 hours.

Nutritional analysis per muffin:

200	Calories	2 %	Calories from Fat
3 g	Protein	3 g	Fiber
47 g	Carbohydrates	107 mg	Sodium
0 g	Fat	0 mg	Cholesterol

Refrigerator Raisin Bran Muffins

These muffins are a delicious way to add fiber to any meal. The batter can be kept in a covered container in the refrigerator for up to 6 weeks.

24 muffins

4 1/2 cups raisin bran cereal
2 1/4 cups unbleached flour
1 cup sugar
2 1/2 teaspoons baking soda
1/2 teaspoon salt
2 cups buttermilk
1/2 cup prune lekvar
2 egg whites

Preheat oven to 400 degrees.

Combine cereal, flour, sugar, baking soda, and salt in a large mixing bowl.

Combine buttermilk, lekvar, and egg whites in a small bowl and blend well. Add buttermilk mixture to dry ingredients and mix with a fork until just blended. Spoon batter just to the tops of muffin cups that have been coated with vegetable spray. Bake for 25 minutes, or until muffins spring back when lightly touched with fingertip. Immediately remove muffins from pan. When muffins are cool, store in an airtight container. The muffins taste best when allowed to sit for 24 hours.

Nutritional analysis per muffin:

126	Calories	3 %	Calories from Fat
3 g	Protein	2 g	Fiber
29 g	Carbohydrates	210 mg	Sodium
1 g	Fat	1 mg	Cholesterol

Sweet Potato Muffins

Serve these as part of an assortment of muffins at Thanksgiving dinner. They are bound to be a favorite.

12 muffins

2 1/4 cups unbleached flour
1 cup sugar
2 teaspoons baking powder
1/4 teaspoon salt
1 teaspoon cinnamon
1/2 teaspoon nutmeg
1/2 cup raisins
1 can (16 ounces) sweet potatoes, drained
1 jar (6 ounces) pear baby food
1 cup skim milk
2 egg whites

Preheat oven to 400 degrees.

Combine flour, sugar, baking powder, salt, cinnamon, nutmeg, and raisins in a large mixing bowl.

In work bowl of food processor, process sweet potatoes until finely chopped. Add pears, milk, and egg whites and process until smooth. Add sweet potato mixture to dry ingredients and mix with a fork until just blended. Spoon batter just to the tops of muffin cups that have been coated with vegetable spray. Bake for 20 to 25 minutes, or until golden brown. Immediately remove muffins from pan. When muffins are cool, store in an airtight container. The muffins taste best when allowed to sit for 24 hours.

Nutritional analysis per muffin:

228	Calories	2 %	Calories from Fat
5 g	Protein	2 g	Fiber
52 g	Carbohydrates	143 mg	Sodium
1 g	Fat	0 mg	Cholesterol

Zucchini Muffins

Enjoy the bounty of your garden by making these delicious zucchini muffins. They are spicy and moist, and the flavor will linger long after the first bite.

12 muffins

2 cups unbleached flour
1/2 cup sugar
1 tablespoon baking powder
1/4 teaspoon baking soda
1/4 teaspoon salt
2 teaspoons cinnamon
3/4 pound zucchini, finely chopped (1 1/2 cups)
1 cup buttermilk
1/4 cup pear baby food
1 egg white
1 teaspoon vanilla

Preheat oven to 400 degrees.

Combine flour, sugar, baking powder, baking soda, salt, and cinnamon in a large mixing bowl.

Combine zucchini, buttermilk, pears, egg white, and vanilla in a small bowl and blend well. Add zucchini mixture to dry ingredients and mix with a fork until just blended. Spoon batter just to the tops of muffin cups that have been coated with vegetable spray. Bake for 25 minutes, or until golden brown. Immediately remove muffins from pan. When muffins are cool, store in an airtight container. The muffins taste best when allowed to sit for 24 hours.

Nutritional analysis per muffin:

127	Calories	3 %	Calories from Fat
3 g	Protein	1 g	Fiber
27 g	Carbohydrates	161 mg	Sodium
0 g	Fat	1 mg	Cholesterol

Layer Cakes, Cheesecakes, Puddings, and Other Desserts

Apple Pudding

*This pudding is a wonderful way to welcome the cool days of autumn.
Serve it plain or with a scoop of nonfat frozen yogurt.*

8 servings

1/3 cup bread crumbs
1 tablespoon sugar
1 cup sugar
1 package dry yeast
1/3 cup unbleached flour
1/2 teaspoon apple pie spice
3 egg whites
1/2 cup skim milk
2 tablespoons apple juice
3 pounds Delicious apples, peeled, cored, and thinly sliced

Preheat oven to 375 degrees.

Combine bread crumbs and 1 tablespoon sugar in a small bowl.
Coat a 1 1/2-quart soufflé dish with vegetable spray and sprinkle
bread crumbs over bottom and sides. Shake out excess crumbs.
Set aside.

Combine 1 cup sugar, yeast, flour, and apple pie spice in a
small bowl.

Combine egg whites, milk, and apple juice in a large mixing
bowl. Add apples and mix well. Add dry ingredients to apple mixture and blend well. Spoon apple mixture into prepared soufflé
dish and bake for 1 hour and 30 minutes, pressing down on apples with the back of a spoon every 30 minutes. Serve warm or at
room temperature.

Nutritional analysis per serving:

249	Calories	4 %	Calories from Fat
4 g	Protein	4 g	Fiber
60 g	Carbohydrates	60 mg	Sodium
1 g	Fat	0 mg	Cholesterol

Apple Tart

10 servings

3 medium-size Granny Smith apples, peeled, cored,
   and thinly sliced
1/4 cup firmly packed dark brown sugar
2 tablespoons Calvados or Grand Marnier
1 1/2 teaspoons cinnamon
1 1/4 cups unbleached flour
1/2 cup granulated sugar
1 teaspoon baking powder
1/8 teaspoon salt
1/2 cup skim milk
1/4 cup applesauce baby food
1 egg white
3/4 teaspoon vanilla

Preheat oven to 350 degrees.

Stir together the apples, brown sugar, Calvados, and cinnamon in
a large mixing bowl until the apple slices are evenly coated. Set
aside.

Combine flour, sugar, baking powder, and salt in a large mixing
bowl.

Combine milk, applesauce, egg white, and vanilla in a small
bowl and blend well. Add applesauce mixture to dry ingredients
and stir with a fork until blended. Pour batter into a 9-inch springform pan that has been coated with vegetable spray. Arrange
overlapping apple slices decoratively on top of batter and drizzle
with any remaining brown sugar mixture that is left in the bowl.
Bake for 40 to 45 minutes, or until cake tester inserted into center of tart comes out clean. Serve warm or at room temperature.

Nutritional analysis per serving:

147	Calories	2 %	Calories from Fat
2 g	Protein	1 g	Fiber
33 g	Carbohydrates	70 mg	Sodium
0 g	Fat	0 mg	Cholesterol

Banana Cake with Chocolate Frosting

My mother was a fabulous baker. Of the family desserts she made, one of my favorites was banana cake with chocolate frosting. This is a low-fat variation of her recipe with the addition of crushed pineapple.

16 servings

Banana Cake
2 1/2 cups unbleached flour
1/2 cup granulated sugar
1 teaspoon baking soda
1/2 teaspoon baking powder
1/4 teaspoon salt
1 jar (6 ounces) pear baby food
3 medium-size ripe bananas, mashed
2 tablespoons plain nonfat yogurt
1 egg
1 egg white
1 1/2 teaspoons vanilla
1 can (8 ounces) unsweetened crushed pineapple, drained

Chocolate Frosting
3 tablespoons light margarine
2 tablespoons Dutch process cocoa
1 1/4 cups powdered sugar
1 teaspoon vanilla

Preheat oven to 350 degrees.

To make banana cake: Combine flour, granulated sugar, baking soda, baking powder, and salt in a large mixing bowl.

Combine pears, bananas, yogurt, egg, egg white, 1 1/2 teaspoons vanilla, and pineapple in work bowl of food processor and blend well. Add banana mixture to dry ingredients and stir with a fork until blended. Spoon batter into two 9-inch round cake pans that have been coated with vegetable spray. Bake for 20 to 25 minutes, or until cake tester inserted into center of cakes comes out clean. Cover cakes with waxed paper and cool on cake racks for 10 minutes. Remove cakes from pans, recover with waxed paper, and cool completely.

To make chocolate frosting: Place margarine in mixing bowl of electric mixer and beat well. Add cocoa, powdered sugar, and 1 teaspoon vanilla and beat until light and fluffy.

When ready to assemble cake: Set first cake layer on a 9-inch cardboard round or cake plate. Place 3-inch strips of waxed paper under edges of cake (this will prevent frosting from getting on clean plate). Spread cake with a layer of chocolate frosting. Place second cake layer on top of first and spread top and sides with remaining frosting. Remove waxed paper strips and refrigerate cake for several hours or overnight. Bring to room temperature before serving.

Note: To decorate cake with rosettes, reserve 1/2 cup of the frosting. Spoon reserved frosting into a pastry bag fitted with a star tip and pipe rosettes around top edge of cake.

Nutritional analysis per serving:

Cake:

141	Calories	6 %	Calories from Fat
3 g	Protein	1 g	Fiber
30 g	Carbohydrates	105 mg	Sodium
1 g	Fat	13 mg	Cholesterol

Frosting:

50	Calories	36 %	Calories from Fat
0 g	Protein	0 g	Fiber
8 g	Carbohydrates	31 mg	Sodium
2 g	Fat	0 mg	Cholesterol

Total:

191	Calories	14 %	Calories from Fat
3 g	Protein	1 g	Fiber
38 g	Carbohydrates	136 mg	Sodium
3 g	Fat	13 mg	Cholesterol

Citrus Bread Pudding

This recipe appears courtesy of the California Prune Board.

6 servings

1 3/4 cups nonfat milk
6 tablespoons egg substitute
6 tablespoons sugar
2 teaspoons vanilla
1 teaspoon *each* grated orange peel and lemon peel
1/2 teaspoon cinnamon
5 cups soft 3/4-inch French bread cubes
3/4 cup (about 4 1/2 ounces) diced pitted prunes
1 tablespoon margarine, melted

In large bowl whisk milk, egg substitute, sugar, vanilla, orange and lemon peel, and cinnamon; stir in bread and prunes. Let stand at room temperature 45 minutes.

Preheat oven to 350 degrees.

Stir margarine into bread mixture; spoon into 8-inch square baking dish coated with vegetable spray. Bake for 45 minutes, or until cake tester inserted into center of pudding comes out clean. Serve warm or at room temperature with warm Citrus Sauce.

To make Citrus Sauce: In small saucepan over medium heat mix 1/2 cup orange juice, 3 tablespoons sugar, 1 tablespoon margarine, 1/4 teaspoon grated lemon peel, and a dash of cinnamon until sugar dissolves. Add 1/4 cup water mixed with 2 teaspoons cornstarch. Bring to boil; stir constantly about 2 minutes, until sauce is slightly thickened. Serve warm.

224	Calories	13 %	Calories from Fat
7 g	Protein	3 g	Fiber
42 g	Carbohydrates	224 mg	Sodium
3 g	Fat	2 mg	Cholesterol

Cottage Cheese Cheesecake

Serve this delicious cheesecake either plain or with fresh fruit, or top it with a strawberry, blueberry, or cherry glaze.

16 servings

Crust
1/4 cup Grape-nuts
2 teaspoons cinnamon
1 tablespoon sugar

Filling
2 cartons (16 ounces each) 1% milk-fat cottage cheese
1 cup egg substitute
1/2 cup evaporated skim milk
1 cup sugar
2 tablespoons unbleached flour
1 tablespoon vanilla

Preheat oven to 350 degrees.

To make crust: Combine Grape-nuts, cinnamon, and 1 tablespoon sugar in a small bowl. Coat a 9-inch springform pan with vegetable spray and sprinkle grape-nut mixture over bottom. Set aside.

To make filling: In work bowl of food processor, process cottage cheese until smooth. Add egg substitute, milk, 1 cup sugar, flour, and vanilla and process until smooth. Pour mixture into prepared springform pan and bake for 1 hour and 25 minutes, or until knife inserted into center of cheesecake comes out clean. Turn off heat and leave cheesecake in oven for 30 minutes. Remove cheesecake from oven and cool to room temperature on a cake rack. Refrigerate for several hours before serving.

Note: To prevent cheesecake from cracking, place a pan of water on bottom shelf of oven while cheesecake is baking.

Nutritional analysis per serving:

Crust:

8	Calories	0 %	Calories from Fat
0 g	Protein	0 g	Fiber
2 g	Carbohydrates	13 mg	Sodium
0 g	Fat	0 mg	Cholesterol

Filling:

105	Calories	8 %	Calories from Fat
8 g	Protein	0 g	Fiber
16 g	Carbohydrates	244 mg	Sodium
1 g	Fat	3 mg	Cholesterol

Total:

113	Calories	8 %	Calories from Fat
8 g	Protein	0 g	Fiber
18 g	Carbohydrates	257 mg	Sodium
1 g	Fat	3 mg	Cholesterol

Crepes with Strawberry Sauce

This dessert lends itself to any kind of sauce. I have served the crepes with a chilled pear coulis or filled with vanilla nonfat yogurt and topped with a raspberry sauce.

8 servings

Crepes

1 1/2 cups skim milk
2 tablespoons pear baby food
1 tablespoon sugar
1/4 cup egg substitute
1 1/4 cups flour

Strawberry Sauce

1 pint fresh strawberries, stems removed
1/4 cup sugar
1 tablespoon *each* pear baby food and fresh lemon juice
1 pint strawberries, sliced
1 tablespoon Royale Chambord liqueur

To make crepes: Combine milk, pears, 1 tablespoon sugar, and egg substitute in a medium-size bowl and blend well. Add flour and mix with a fork until just blended.

Place a 7-inch nonstick pan that has been sprayed with butter-flavored vegetable spray on moderate heat. When pan is hot, pour 1/4 cup crepe mixture in pan, quickly tilting pan in all directions, until the crepe makes a circle (it is okay if it does not completely cover the surface of the pan or is not perfectly round). Cook the crepe for 1 minute, or until it can be shaken loose from pan. Turn crepe over and cook for about 30 seconds more, or just until bottom is firm. Do not let it brown. Cool crepe on a towel while making the remaining 15 crepes, lightly coating pan with vegetable spray each time. As the crepes cool, they can be stacked on top of each other by placing a piece of waxed paper between each layer. If not serving the crepes right away, store them in an airtight container.

To make strawberry sauce: In work bowl of food processor, process 1 pint strawberries until smooth. Add ¼ cup sugar, pears, and lemon juice and process until smooth. Transfer mixture to a small heavy saucepan and cook over moderate heat until it comes to a boil, stirring constantly. Add strawberry slices and Chambord to saucepan and cook just until it begins to boil.

When ready to serve, fold crepe in half, and fold in half again. Place 2 crepes on each plate and top with 2 to 3 tablespoons strawberry sauce.

Nutritional analysis per serving:

Crepes:

96	Calories	3 %	Calories from Fat
4 g	Protein	1 g	Fiber
19 g	Carbohydrates	27 mg	Sodium
0 g	Fat	1 mg	Cholesterol

Sauce:

61	Calories	5 %	Calories from Fat
1 g	Protein	2 g	Fiber
14 g	Carbohydrates	1 mg	Sodium
0 g	Fat	0 mg	Cholesterol

Total:

157	Calories	6 %	Calories from Fat
5 g	Protein	3 g	Fiber
33 g	Carbohydrates	28 mg	Sodium
1 g	Fat	1 mg	Cholesterol

Everyone's Favorite
Peanut Butter Cake

No matter how old you are, peanut butter is an all-time favorite. This prize-winning cake is made with peanut butter in both the cake and the frosting, and the intensity of its flavor is enjoyed with every bite.

12 servings

Peanut Butter Cake
2 1/4 cups unbleached flour
1/2 cup firmly packed dark brown sugar
6 tablespoons granulated sugar
1 tablespoon baking powder
1/4 teaspoon salt
1 jar (6 ounces) pear baby food
1/4 cup creamy peanut butter
2 egg whites
2/3 cup skim milk
1/2 cup plain nonfat yogurt
1 tablespoon vanilla

Peanut Butter Frosting
4 ounces Neufchâtel or light cream cheese, at room
   temperature
2 tablespoons peanut butter
1 1/2 cups powdered sugar
1 teaspoon vanilla

Preheat oven to 350 degrees.

To make peanut butter cake: Combine flour, granulated and brown sugars, baking powder, and salt in a large mixing bowl.

Combine pears, 1/4 cup peanut butter, egg whites, milk, yogurt, and 1 tablespoon vanilla in a small bowl and blend well. Add peanut butter mixture to dry ingredients and mix with a fork until blended. Spoon batter into two 8-inch round cake pans that have been coated with vegetable spray. Bake for 25 to 30 minutes, or until cake tester inserted into center of cake comes out clean. Cover cakes with waxed paper and cool on cake racks. When cool, remove cakes from pans and ice with peanut butter frosting.

To make peanut butter frosting: Combine cream cheese and 2 tablespoons peanut butter in bowl of electric mixer; beat until smooth. Add powdered sugar and 1 teaspoon vanilla and beat until blended.

When ready to assemble cake: Set first cake layer on an 8-inch cardboard round or cake plate. Place 3-inch strips of waxed paper under edges of cake (this will prevent frosting from getting on clean plate). Spread a thin layer of frosting on cake layer, top with second cake layer, and spread frosting over top and sides of cake. Remove waxed paper strips and refrigerate cake for several hours. Bring cake to room temperature before serving.

Note: Try making this cake with the new reduced-fat peanut butters that are now available.

Nutritional analysis per serving:

Cake:

195	Calories	14 %	Calories from Fat
5 g	Protein	1 g	Fiber
37 g	Carbohydrates	169 mg	Sodium
3 g	Fat	1 mg	Cholesterol

Frosting:

96	Calories	38 %	Calories from Fat
2 g	Protein	0 g	Fiber
13 g	Carbohydrates	51 mg	Sodium
4 g	Fat	7 mg	Cholesterol

Total:

291	Calories	22 %	Calories from Fat
7 g	Protein	1 g	Fiber
50 g	Carbohydrates	220 mg	Sodium
7 g	Fat	8 mg	Cholesterol

Honey Graham-Cracker Cake

The graham cracker was developed during the religious movement called Grahamism, which was popular throughout New England in the 1830s to 1840s. Reverend Sylvester Graham preached against white bread, flour, and cereals, among many other things, and encouraged his followers, called Grahamites, to use coarse bran. In an effort to appease Reverend Graham, town bakers developed a line of whole wheat products, including the graham cracker. Today, one of my favorite ways to eat them is in this delicious layer cake.

12 servings

Honey Graham-Cracker Cake
22 double graham crackers, finely ground
1 tablespoon baking powder
1 cup granulated sugar
1 jar (6 ounces) pear baby food
4 egg whites
1 cup skim milk
1 tablespoon vanilla

Whip Cream Frosting
1 carton (8 ounces) frozen nondairy whip cream, defrosted
2 tablespoons powdered sugar
2 tablespoons coffee liqueur

Preheat oven to 350 degrees.

To make honey graham-cracker cake: Combine graham crackers, baking powder, and granulated sugar in a large mixing bowl.

Combine pears, egg whites, milk, and vanilla in a small bowl and blend well. Add pear mixture to dry ingredients and mix with a fork until blended. Spoon batter into two 8-inch round cake pans that have been coated with vegetable spray and lightly dusted with flour. Bake for 22 to 26 minutes, or until cake tester inserted into center of cake comes out clean. Cover cakes with waxed paper and cool on a cake rack.

To make whip cream frosting: Combine whip cream, powdered sugar, and coffee liqueur in bowl of electric mixer and beat until light and fluffy.

When ready to assemble cake: Set first cake layer on an 8-inch cardboard round or cake plate. Place 3-inch strips of waxed paper under cake (this will prevent frosting from getting on clean plate). Spread a thick layer of frosting on first cake layer, then top with second layer. Frost top and sides of cake with remaining frosting. Remove waxed paper strips and refrigerate cake for several hours.

Note: To decorate cake with rosettes, reserve 1/2 cup frosting. Spoon reserved frosting into a pastry bag fitted with a small star tip and pipe rosettes around top edge of cake.

Nutritional analysis per serving:

Cake:

199	Calories	14 %	Calories from Fat
4 g	Protein	1 g	Fiber
39 g	Carbohydrates	274 mg	Sodium
3 g	Fat	4 mg	Cholesterol

Frosting:

43	Calories	63 %	Calories from Fat
0 g	Protein	0 g	Fiber
4 g	Carbohydrates	7 mg	Sodium
3 g	Fat	0 mg	Cholesterol

Total:

242	Calories	22 %	Calories from Fat
4 g	Protein	1 g	Fiber
43 g	Carbohydrates	281 mg	Sodium ·
6 g	Fat	4 mg	Cholesterol

Italian Cream Cake

This cake makes the perfect grand finale to an Italian dinner. For a decorative look, pipe rosettes on the top edge of the cake or top it with eight caramelized walnuts.

12 servings

Cake
2 cups unbleached flour
1 cup granulated sugar
1/2 cup finely chopped walnuts
1 teaspoon baking soda
1 cup buttermilk
1 jar (6 ounces) pear baby food
5 egg whites
1 teaspoon vanilla

Cream Cheese Frosting
4 ounces Neufchâtel or light cream cheese, at
    room temperature
1 cup powdered sugar
1/2 teaspoon vanilla

Preheat oven to 350 degrees.

To make cake: Combine flour, granulated sugar, walnuts, and baking soda in a large mixing bowl.

Combine buttermilk, pears, egg whites, and 1 teaspoon vanilla in a small bowl and blend well. Add pear mixture to dry ingredients and mix with a fork until blended. Spoon batter evenly into two 8-inch round cake pans that have been coated with vegetable spray. Bake for 20 to 25 minutes, or until cake tester inserted into center of cakes come out clean. Cover cakes with waxed paper and cool on cake racks for 15 minutes. Remove cake from pans, recover with waxed paper, and cool completely.

To make cream cheese frosting: Place cream cheese in mixing bowl of electric mixer; beat just until blended. Add powdered sugar and 1/2 teaspoon vanilla and beat until light and fluffy.

When ready to assemble to cake: Set first cake layer on an 8-inch cardboard round or cake plate and spread with half of the cream cheese frosting. Top with second cake layer and spread with remaining frosting. Refrigerate cake several hours or overnight. Bring to room temperature before serving.

Note: For an added touch, reserve 1/2 cup frosting. Spoon reserved frosting into a pastry bag fitted with a star tip and pipe rosettes around top edge of cake.

Nutritional analysis per serving:

Cake:

200	Calories	18 %	Calories from Fat
5 g	Protein	1 g	Fiber
36 g	Carbohydrates	115 mg	Sodium
4 g	Fat	1 mg	Cholesterol

Frosting:

58	Calories	31 %	Calories from Fat
1 g	Protein	0 g	Fiber
9 g	Carbohydrates	38 mg	Sodium
2 g	Fat	7 mg	Cholesterol

Total:

258	Calories	21 %	Calories from Fat
6 g	Protein	1 g	Fiber
45 g	Carbohydrates	152 mg	Sodium
6 g	Fat	8 mg	Cholesterol

Lemon Ice-Box Cake

This is an exceptional dessert to serve during the long, hot days of summer. It is a light, refreshing, and fantastically delicious combination of ladyfingers, strawberries, and lemon mousse.

10 servings

Ladyfingers
1 cup unbleached flour
1/2 cup sugar
1 1/2 teaspoons baking powder
1/8 teaspoon salt
1/3 cup buttermilk
1 egg
1 egg white
1/4 cup pear baby food
1 tablespoon canola oil
1 teaspoon vanilla

Lemon Mousse
3/4 cup sugar
2 tablespoons cornstarch
1 teaspoon unflavored gelatin
1/8 teaspoon salt
1 cup cold water
1/4 cup egg substitute
6 tablespoons fresh lemon juice
1 teaspoon finely grated lemon peel
1 cup vanilla nonfat yogurt

1 pint fresh strawberries, sliced

Preheat oven to 350 degrees.

To make ladyfingers: Combine flour, 1/2 cup sugar, baking powder, and salt in a medium-size bowl.

Combine buttermilk, egg, egg white, pears, oil, and vanilla in a small bowl and blend well. Add buttermilk mixture to dry ingredients and mix with a fork until blended. Spoon batter into an 8-inch square baking pan that has been coated with vegetable spray. Bake for 20 minutes, or until a cake tester inserted into center of cake comes out clean. Cover cake with waxed paper and cool on a cake rack. Remove cake from pan to cool completely.

To make lemon mousse: Combine 3/4 cup sugar, cornstarch, gelatin, salt, and water in a medium-size saucepan over moderate heat. Cook for 10 to 15 minutes, or until thick, stirring frequently. Reduce heat to low, cover saucepan, and cook for 10 minutes. Add egg substitute and blend with a whisk until smooth (it is okay if there is some egg white showing). Cook for 10 minutes, uncovered, stirring occasionally. Remove saucepan from heat and add lemon juice and lemon peel; cool to room temperature. When lemon filling is cool, add vanilla yogurt and blend well.

When ready to assemble cake: Slice the cake horizontally into 2 layers (it is okay if they are uneven). Cut each layer in 4 squares and each of those squares into 4 ladyfingers. There should be 32 ladyfingers altogether.

Place 16 ladyfingers on the bottom of a 1 1/2-quart soufflé dish. Top with half of the strawberry slices and half of the lemon mousse. Repeat with the remaining ladyfingers, strawberries, and lemon mousse. Refrigerate cake for several hours, covering dish with plastic wrap after the cake is firm.

Nutritional analysis per serving:

Cake:

114	Calories	16 %	Calories from Fat
3 g	Protein	0 g	Fiber
21 g	Carbohydrates	102 mg	Sodium
2 g	Fat	22 mg	Cholesterol

Mousse:

108	Calories	0 %	Calories from Fat
3 g	Protein	1 g	Fiber
24 g	Carbohydrates	75 mg	Sodium
0 g	Fat	1 mg	Cholesterol

Total:

222	Calories	8 %	Calories from Fat
6 g	Protein	1 g	Fiber
45 g	Carbohydrates	177 mg	Sodium
2 g	Fat	23 mg	Cholesterol

Lemon Mousse

Although this dessert is not made with puréed fruit to substitute for fat, I have included it because it is very low in fat, yet deliciously light and refreshing.

8 servings

1 envelope plain gelatin
1 tablespoon cold water
1/2 cup fresh lemon juice
1 cup sugar
1 tablespoon finely grated lemon peel
3/4 cup vanilla nonfat yogurt
6 egg whites, at room temperature
crystallized violets for garnish (optional)
mint sprigs for garnish (optional)

Sprinkle gelatin over cold water in a small, heavy saucepan. Add lemon juice and sugar and blend well. Cook over moderate heat for 5 to 6 minutes, or until gelatin dissolves, stirring occasionally. Boil for 1 minute. Add lemon peel and refrigerate until mixture is the consistency of egg whites.

Transfer lemon mixture to a large mixing bowl and add vanilla yogurt; blend well. In bowl of electric mixer, beat egg whites until stiff peaks form but are not dry. Fold egg whites into lemon mixture until just blended. Spoon lemon mousse into wine goblets or sherbet dishes and refrigerate for several hours, or until firm. Garnish each serving with a crystallized violet and a sprig of mint, if desired.

Nutritional analysis per serving:

128	Calories	1 %	Calories from Fat
5 g	Protein	0 g	Fiber
28 g	Carbohydrates	59 mg	Sodium
0 g	Fat	0 mg	Cholesterol

Oatmeal Cake with Maple Syrup Meringue

This is an adaption of a recipe that was featured in a Washington Post *article on the Firehook Bakery and Coffee House located in Alexandria, Va. Firehook is renowned for its delicious varieties of breads and baked goods.*

12 servings

Oatmeal Cake
1 cup boiling water
3/4 cup rolled oats or quick-cooking oats
1 1/2 cups unbleached flour
3/4 cup *each* firmly packed light brown sugar and
    granulated sugar
1 teaspoon baking soda
1/4 teaspoon salt
3/4 teaspoon cinnamon
1/4 teaspoon nutmeg
1/4 cup pear baby food
2 egg whites
1 teaspoon vanilla

Meringue
1 cup maple syrup
3 egg whites

chopped pecans or walnuts for garnish (optional)

Preheat oven to 350 degrees.

To make oatmeal cake: Pour boiling water over oats, cover, and let stand 20 minutes.

Combine flour, sugars, baking soda, salt, cinnamon, and nutmeg in a large mixing bowl.

Combine pears, 2 egg whites, and vanilla in a small bowl and blend well. Add pear mixture and oatmeal to dry ingredients and mix with a fork until blended. Spoon batter into two 9-inch round cake pans that have been coated with vegetable spray and lightly dusted with flour. Bake for 25 to 30 minutes, or until cake tester inserted into center of cakes comes out clean. Cover cakes with waxed paper and cool on cake racks.

To make meringue: Boil maple syrup to firm-ball stage (248 degrees on a candy thermometer). Beat 3 egg whites until they form stiff peaks but are not dry. Gradually add hot maple syrup to beaten egg whites and beat until fluffy.

To assemble cake: Set first cake layer on a 9-inch cardboard round or cake plate. Place 3-inch strips of waxed paper under edges of cake (this will prevent any frosting from getting on clean plate). Spread a thick layer of meringue on first layer. Place second layer on top and frost top and sides of cake with remaining meringue. Garnish with toasted nuts. Remove and discard waxed paper strips.

Nutritional analysis per serving:

Cake:

184	Calories	3 %	Calories from Fat
3 g	Protein	1 g	Fiber
42 g	Carbohydrates	128 mg	Sodium
1 g	Fat	0 mg	Cholesterol

Meringue:

71	Calories	0 %	Calories from Fat
1 g	Protein	0 g	Fiber
17 g	Carbohydrates	16 mg	Sodium
0 g	Fat	0 mg	Cholesterol

Total:

255	Calories	2 %	Calories from Fat
4 g	Protein	1 g	Fiber
59 g	Carbohydrates	144 mg	Sodium
1 g	Fat	0 mg	Cholesterol

Orange Layer Cake

This sensational cake is made of two orange-flavored cake layers and filled and frosted with a heavenly orange frosting. Best of all, it has only 1 gram of fat per serving!

12 servings

Orange Cake
2 cups bread flour
1 cup granulated sugar
1 tablespoon baking powder
1/4 teaspoon salt
1 tablespoon finely grated orange peel
1 jar (6 ounces) pear baby food
3/4 cup skim milk
1/4 cup fresh orange juice
1/2 teaspoon orange extract
4 egg whites, at room temperature
2 tablespoons granulated sugar

Orange Frosting
2 tablespoons light margarine
2 cups powdered sugar
2 tablespoons fresh orange juice
1 teaspoon finely grated orange peel
1 teaspoon orange extract
1 cup powdered sugar

Preheat oven to 350 degreees.

To make orange cake: Combine flour, 1 cup granulated sugar, baking powder, salt, and orange peel in a large mixing bowl.

Combine pears, milk, 1/4 cup orange juice, and 1/2 teaspoon orange extract in a small bowl and blend well.

In mixing bowl of electric mixer on medium speed, beat egg whites until soft peaks form. Add 2 tablespoons granulated sugar and beat egg whites until stiff peaks form but are not dry. Add orange juice mixture to egg whites and beat on moderately low speed until blended. Add egg white mixture to dry ingredients and quickly mix with a fork until blended (it may be necessary to complete the mixing by using a rubber spatula to quickly fold in). Pour batter into two 8-inch round cake pans that have been coated with vegetable spray. Bake for 25 to 30 minutes, or until cake tester inserted into center of cakes comes out clean. Cover cakes with waxed paper and cool on cake racks.

To make orange frosting: In mixing bowl of electric mixer, beat margarine until smooth. Add 2 cups powdered sugar, 2 tablespoons orange juice, orange peel, and 1 teaspoon orange extract and beat until blended. Add 1 cup powdered sugar and beat until orange frosting is light and fluffy.

When ready to assemble cake: Set first cake layer on an 8-inch cardboard round or cake plate. Place 3-inch strips of waxed paper under edges of cake (this will prevent frosting from getting on clean plate). Spread a layer of frosting on first cake layer, place second cake layer on top and frost top and sides of cake. Remove waxed paper strips and refrigerate cake for several hours. Serve slightly chilled.

Nutritional analysis per serving:

Cake:

171	Calories	2 %	Calories from Fat
4 g	Protein	1 g	Fiber
38 g	Carbohydrates	145 mg	Sodium
0 g	Fat	0 mg	Cholesterol

Frosting:

103	Calories	6 %	Calories from Fat
0 g	Protein	0 g	Fiber
25 g	Carbohydrates	9 mg	Sodium
1 g	Fat	0 mg	Cholesterol

Total:

274	Calories	3 %	Calories from Fat
4 g	Protein	1 g	Fiber
63 g	Carbohydrates	154 mg	Sodium
1 g	Fat	0 mg	Cholesterol

Orange-Scented Buttermilk Cake

This dessert consists of a layer of yellow cake brushed with a Grand Marnier syrup then iced with a silky chocolate glaze. Top with chocolate curls for an especially dramatic presentation.

12 servings

Grand Marnier Syrup
2 tablespoons sugar
2 tablespoons water
2 1/2 to 3 tablespoons Grand Marnier

Buttermilk Cake
1 cup bread flour
1/2 cup sugar
1/2 tablespoon baking powder
1/4 teaspoon salt
1/3 cup buttermilk
1 egg
1 egg white
1/4 cup pear baby food
1 tablespoon canola oil
1 teaspoon vanilla

Chocolate Glaze
3/4 cup chocolate chips
3 tablespoons liquid nondairy creamer
1 tablespoon light corn syrup

Chocolate curls (page 274, optional)
Powdered sugar (optional)

To make Grand Marnier syrup: Combine 2 tablespoons sugar and water in a small saucepan over moderately high heat and bring to a rolling boil. Remove saucepan from heat, cover, and bring to room temperature. Add Grand Marnier and blend well. Set aside.

Preheat oven to 350 degrees.

To make buttermilk cake: Combine flour, 1/2 cup sugar, baking powder, and salt in a large mixing bowl.

Combine buttermilk, egg, egg white, pears, oil, and vanilla in a small bowl and blend well. Add buttermilk mixture to dry ingredients and mix with a fork until blended. Spoon batter into a 9-inch round cake pan that has been coated with vegetable spray. Bake for 20 to 25 minutes, or until cake tester inserted into center of cake comes out clean. Cover cake with waxed paper and cool on a cake rack for 10 minutes. Remove cake from pan, recover with waxed paper, and cool completely. Pierce top of cake with a fork several times and brush with Grand Marnier syrup. Set aside.

To make chocolate glaze: Place chocolate chips, creamer, and corn syrup in a small heavy saucepan, covered, over low heat. Cook just until chocolate is soft enough to blend.

When ready to assemble cake: Set cake layer on a 9-inch cardboard round or cake plate. Place 3-inch strips of waxed paper under edges of cake (this will prevent glaze from getting on clean plate). Spread glaze over top and sides of cake. Remove waxed paper strips and store cake in an airtight container.

To decorate cake: Place chocolate curls on top of cake. To create stripes, place six to eight 1/2-inch strips of waxed paper equally spaced over chocolate curls and dust with powdered sugar; carefully remove the waxed paper strips.

Nutritional analysis per serving:

Syrup:

16	Calories	0 %	Calories from Fat
0 g	Protein	0 g	Fiber
4 g	Carbohydrates	0 mg	Sodium
0 g	Fat	0 mg	Cholesterol

Cake:

94	Calories	19 %	Calories from Fat
2 g	Protein	0 g	Fiber
17 g	Carbohydrates	235 mg	Sodium
2 g	Fat	18 mg	Cholesterol

Glaze:

77	Calories	58 %	Calories from Fat
0 g	Protein	1 g	Fiber
8 g	Carbohydrates	5 mg	Sodium
5 g	Fat	0 mg	Cholesterol

Total:

187	Calories	34 %	Calories from Fat
2 g	Protein	1 g	Fiber
29 g	Carbohydrates	240 mg	Sodium
7 g	Fat	18 mg	Cholesterol

Peach Pudding

For a special treat, top this simple dessert with a scoop of peach nonfat frozen yogurt.

8 servings

1/3 cup bread crumbs
1 tablespoon sugar
1 cup sugar
1 package dry yeast
1/3 cup unbleached flour
1/2 teaspoon cinnamon
2 egg whites
1/2 cup skim milk
2 tablespoons peach baby food
1 tablespoon finely grated lemon peel
2 packages (16 ounces each) frozen peach slices, defrosted, or
    4 peaches, peeled and sliced (about 4 cups)

Preheat oven to 375 degrees.

Combine bread crumbs and 1 tablespoon sugar in a small bowl. Coat a 1 1/2-quart soufflé dish with vegetable spray and sprinkle bread crumbs over bottom and sides. Shake out excess crumbs. Set aside.

Combine 1 cup sugar, yeast, flour, and cinnamon in a small bowl.

Combine egg whites, milk, peach baby food, and lemon peel in a large mixing bowl. Add peaches and mix well. Add dry ingredients to peach mixture and blend well. Spoon peach mixture into prepared soufflé dish and bake for 1 hour and 30 minutes, pressing down on peaches with the back of a spoon every 30 minutes. Serve warm or at room temperature.

Nutritional analysis per serving:

256	Calories	2 %	Calories from Fat
4 g	Protein	4 g	Fiber
62 g	Carbohydrates	60 mg	Sodium
0 g	Fat	0 mg	Cholesterol

Pineapple Cake

In Hawaii, our family ate at a fabulous restaurant that featured a delicious white cake with pineapple filling, encased in a rich buttercream frosting and topped with toasted coconut. This is my reduced-fat version of this sensational dessert.

16 servings

Pineapple Filling
2 cans (8 ounces each) unsweetened crushed pineapple
3 1/2 teaspoons cornstarch
1 tablespoon granulated sugar
dash of salt
1 cup reserved pineapple juice
1/2 teaspoon vanilla

Cake
2 cups bread flour
3/4 cup granulated sugar
1 tablespoon baking powder
1/4 teaspoon salt
1 jar (6 ounces) pear baby food
1 cup skim milk
1 teaspoon vanilla
4 egg whites
1/4 cup granulated sugar

Frosting
3 tablespoons light margarine
2 cups powdered sugar
1/4 cup reserved pineapple juice
1 cup powdered sugar

To make pineapple filling: Spoon pineapple into a strainer that has been placed over a medium-size bowl. Press pineapple with the back of a spoon to press out 1 1/4 cups of pineapple juice. Reserve 1 cup pineapple juice for the filling and 1/4 cup for the frosting.

Combine cornstarch, 1 tablespoon sugar, and salt in a small heavy saucepan and blend well. Gradually add reserved 1 cup pineapple juice and mix until smooth. Place saucepan over moderate heat and cook until mixture comes to a boil and thickens. Reduce heat and simmer for 2 minutes, stirring occasionally. Remove saucepan from heat and add vanilla and reserved pineapple; blend well. Cool to room temperature. Cover and refrigerate pineapple filling for several hours, or until firm and no longer runny.

Preheat oven to 350 degrees.

To make cake: Combine flour, 3/4 cup granulated sugar, baking powder, and salt in a large mixing bowl.

Combine pears, milk, and vanilla in a small bowl and blend well.

In mixing bowl of electric mixer, beat egg whites on moderate speed until they are foamy. Add 1/4 cup granulated sugar, 1 tablespoon at a time, beating well after each addition. Increase speed to high and beat egg whites until stiff peaks form but are not dry. Add pear mixture to egg whites and beat on moderate speed just to lightly blend. Add pear mixture to dry ingredients and quickly mix with a fork to blend. Pour batter into two 9-inch round cake pans that have been coated with vegetable spray. Bake for 25 minutes, or until cake tester inserted into center of cakes comes out clean. Cover cakes with waxed paper and cool on cake racks for 10 minutes. Remove cakes from pans, recover with waxed paper, and cool completely.

To make frosting: In mixing bowl of electric mixer, beat margarine, 2 cups powdered sugar, and reserved 1/4 cup pineapple juice and beat well. Add 1 cup powdered sugar and beat until light and fluffy.

When ready to assemble cake: Set first cake layer on a cake plate or 9-inch cardboard round. Place 3-inch strips of waxed paper under edges of cake (this will prevent frosting from getting on clean plate). Spread chilled pineapple filling evenly over first layer, leaving about a 1/4-inch border. Place second layer on top of filling and spread frosting over top and sides of cake. Remove and discard waxed paper strips. Refrigerate cake for several hours.

Note: To decorate cake, reserve 1/4 cup pineapple filling and scant 3 tablespoons frosting. Spoon reserved frosting into a small pastry bag fitted with a star tip and pipe rosettes in a small circle on top center of cake and place the reserved pineapple filling in center of rosettes.

Nutritional analysis per serving:

Filling:

28	Calories	0 %	Calories from Fat
0 g	Protein	0 g	Fiber
7 g	Carbohydrates	73 mg	Sodium
0 g	Fat	0 mg	Cholesterol

Cake:

123	Calories	2 %	Calories from Fat
3 g	Protein	0 g	Fiber
27 g	Carbohydrates	110 mg	Sodium
0 g	Fat	0 mg	Cholesterol

Frosting:

84	Calories	11 %	Calories from Fat
0 g	Protein	0 g	Fiber
19 g	Carbohydrates	26 mg	Sodium
1 g	Fat	0 mg	Cholesterol

Total:

235	Calories	4 %	Calories from Fat
3 g	Protein	0 g	Fiber
53 g	Carbohydrates	209 mg	Sodium
1 g	Fat	0 mg	Cholesterol

Pumpkin Cheesecake

This lowfat pumpkin cheesecake is dense, delicious, and delicately spiced. Much of the fat has been reduced by using nonfat cream cheese, lowfat cottage cheese and sour cream, and evaporated skim milk.

12 servings

Crust
3 tablespoons Grape-nuts cereal
1 tablespoon sugar
1/8 teaspoon cinnamon

Pumpkin Cheesecake Filling
2 packages (8 ounces each) nonfat cream cheese, at
    room temperature
1 cup 1% milkfat cottage cheese
1/2 cup lite sour cream
1 heaping cup solid-pack canned pumpkin
3/4 cup sugar
3/4 cup egg substitute
1/2 cup evaporated skim milk
3 tablespoons unbleached flour
2 teaspoons cinnamon
1/2 teaspoon ginger
1/4 teaspoon ground cloves
1 tablespoon vanilla

Apricot Glaze (optional)
1/2 cup apricot preserves
1 tablespoon sugar
1 tablespoon Grand Marnier

Preheat oven to 325 degrees.

To make crust: Combine Grape-nuts, 1 tablespoon sugar, and ⅛ teaspoon cinnamon in a small bowl. Coat an 8-inch springform pan with vegetable spray and sprinkle grape-nut mixture over bottom and sides, allowing excess to remain on bottom. Set aside.

To make pumpkin cheesecake filling: In mixing bowl of electric mixer, beat cream cheese and cottage cheese just until smooth. Add sour cream and pumpkin and blend well. Add ¾ cup sugar, egg substitute, milk, flour, cinnamon, ginger, cloves, and vanilla and blend until smooth. Pour batter into prepared springform pan and bake for 1 hour and 25 minutes, or until knife inserted into center of cheesecake comes out clean. Turn off heat and let cheesecake remain in oven for 30 minutes. Remove cheesecake from oven and cool to room temperature on a cake rack. If not using apricot glaze, refrigerate cheesecake for several hours, or overnight.

To make apricot glaze: Cook apricot preserves in a small heavy saucepan over moderate heat until it comes to a boil. Spoon preserves into a fine sieve placed over a bowl and press down to remove as much liquid as possible; discard pulp. To liquid, add 1 tablespoon sugar and Grand Marnier and blend well. Spread apricot glaze over cheesecake and refrigerate for several hours, or overnight.

Note: To prevent cheesecake from cracking, place a pan filled with water on bottom shelf of oven while cheesecake is baking.

Nutritional analysis per serving:

Cheesecake with crust:

61	Calories	15 %	Calories from Fat
6 g	Protein	1 g	Fiber
7 g	Carbohydrates	164 mg	Sodium
1 g	Fat	3 mg	Cholesterol

Glaze:

32	Calories	0 %	Calories from Fat
0 g	Protein	0 g	Fiber
8 g	Carbohydrates	1 mg	Sodium
0 g	Fat	0 mg	Cholesterol

Total:

93	Calories	10 %	Calories from Fat
6 g	Protein	1 g	Fiber
15 g	Carbohydrates	165 mg	Sodium
1 g	Fat	0 mg	Cholesterol

Pumpkin Flan

This spicy pumpkin flan is a wonderful alternative to the classic flan. I like to serve it plain or with a dollop of nonfat whip cream spiced with ginger.

8 servings

$1/2$ cup sugar
2 tablespoons water
$1/8$ teaspoon cream of tartar
1 cup sugar
1 teaspoon cinnamon
$1/8$ teaspoon nutmeg
$1/8$ teaspoon salt
1 cup solid-pack canned pumpkin
1 can (12 ounces) evaporated skim milk
$3/4$ cup egg substitute
1 tablespoon vanilla

Preheat oven to 350 degrees.

Combine $1/2$ cup sugar, water, and cream of tartar in a small heavy saucepan over moderate heat. Bring to a boil, stirring occasionally. Let boil 10 to 12 minutes, or until sugar melts and turns a rich golden brown. Pour caramel into an 8-inch square baking pan to coat the bottom. Set aside.

Combine 1 cup sugar, cinnamon, nutmeg, and salt in a small bowl.

Combine pumpkin, milk, egg substitute, and vanilla in a large mixing bowl and blend well. Add dry ingredients and blend well. Pour pumpkin mixture into caramel-coated pan. Place this pan into a larger pan and pour hot water into larger pan until it comes halfway up the flan pan. Bake for 1 hour and 10 minutes, or until knife inserted into center of flan comes out clean. Cool flan on cake rack until it comes to room temperature. Refrigerate for several hours. When ready to serve, cut around the sides of pan with a sharp knife and invert pan over a large platter, allowing it to sit for a few minutes so that caramel runs down top and sides of flan. Remove flan from pan and cut into serving pieces.

Nutritional analysis per serving:

206	Calories	2 %	Calories from Fat
5 g	Protein	1 g	Fiber
46 g	Carbohydrates	117 mg	Sodium
0 g	Fat	2 mg	Cholesterol

Pumpkin-Gingerbread Cake

16 servings

Pumpkin-Gingerbread
1 3/4 cups unbleached flour
1/2 cup firmly packed dark brown sugar
1 teaspoon baking soda
2 teaspoons ginger
1/2 teaspoon allspice
1/4 teaspoon cinnamon
1/4 teaspoon salt
1 cup solid-pack canned pumpkin
1 jar (6 ounces) pear baby food
1/2 cup maple syrup
2 tablespoons molasses
2 egg whites
1 teaspoon vanilla

Cream Cheese Frosting
6 ounces Neufchâtel or light cream cheese, at
   room temperature
3 cups powdered sugar
1 teaspoon skim milk
1 teaspoon vanilla

Marzipan pumpkin for decoration (optional)
Orange flower for decoration (optional)

Preheat oven to 350 degrees.

To make pumpkin-gingerbread: Combine flour, brown sugar, baking soda, ginger, allspice, cinnamon, and salt in a large mixing bowl.

Combine pumpkin, pears, maple syrup, molasses, egg whites, and vanilla in a medium-size bowl and blend well. Add pumpkin mixture to dry ingredients and mix with a fork until blended. Pour batter into two 8-inch round cake pans that have been coated with vegetable spray. Bake for 20 to 25 minutes, or until cake tester inserted into center of cakes comes out clean. Cover cakes with waxed paper and cool on cake racks.

To make cream cheese frosting: In mixing bowl of electric mixer, lightly beat cream cheese until just smooth. Add powdered sugar, milk, and vanilla and beat on medium speed until light and fluffy.

When ready to assemble cake: Remove cakes from pans. Set first cake layer on an 8-inch cardboard round or cake plate and place 3-inch strips of waxed paper under edges of cake (this will prevent frosting from getting on clean plate). Spread a layer of frosting on cake layer and top with second cake layer. Frost top and sides of cake with remaining frosting. Remove waxed paper strips and refrigerate cake for several hours.

To decorate cake, reserve 1/2 cup frosting. Spoon reserved frosting into a pastry bag fitted with a star tip. Make a circle in the center of the cake by pressing gently on the top with a drinking glass. Pipe rosettes on the indentation and around top edge of cake. For a dramatic finish, place a marzipan pumpkin or an orange flower in the circle.

Nutritional analysis per serving:

Cake:

117	Calories	3 %	Calories from Fat
3 g	Protein	2 g	Fiber
27 g	Carbohydrates	97 mg	Sodium
1 g	Fat	0 mg	Cholesterol

Frosting:

102	Calories	18 %	Calories from Fat
1 g	Protein	0 g	Fiber
19 g	Carbohydrates	43 mg	Sodium
2 g	Fat	8 mg	Cholesterol

Total:

219	Calories	12 %	Calories from Fat
4 g	Protein	2 g	Fiber
46 g	Carbohydrates	140 mg	Sodium
3 g	Fat	8 mg	Cholesterol

Rum-Apple Cake

8 servings

Apple Cake
1 cup unbleached flour
3/4 cup sugar
1 teaspoon baking soda
1/8 teaspoon salt
1 teaspoon cinnamon
1/2 teaspoon nutmeg
1/4 teaspoon allspice
1/4 cup pear baby food
1 egg white
2 Granny Smith apples, unpeeled and chopped (about 2 cups)

Rum Sauce
1 teaspoon cornstarch
2 tablespoons cold water
1/4 cup pear baby food
1/2 cup sugar
1/4 cup skim milk
1 1/2 tablespoons rum
1/2 teaspoon vanilla
1/8 teaspoon cinnamon

Preheat oven to 400 degrees.

To make apple cake: Combine flour, 3/4 cup sugar, baking soda, salt, 1 teaspoon cinnamon, nutmeg, and allspice in a large mixing bowl.

Combine pears, egg white, and apples in a large mixing bowl. Add apple mixture to dry ingredients and mix with a fork until blended. Spoon batter into an 8-inch square baking pan that has been coated with vegetable spray and bake for 30 to 35 minutes, or until cake is set and golden brown. Immediately cut cake into serving-size pieces.

To make rum sauce: While apple cake is baking, combine cornstarch and water in a small bowl and blend until smooth.

Combine pears, 1/2 cup sugar, milk, and cornstarch mixture in a small heavy saucepan and blend until smooth. Cook over moderate heat for 10 to 12 minutes, or until mixture begins to thicken. Remove saucepan from heat and let sit for 5 minutes. Add rum, vanilla, and 1/8 teaspoon cinnamon and blend well.

When ready to serve: Place a warm piece of apple cake in a dish and spoon a generous amount of warm rum sauce over cake.

Nutritional analysis per serving:

Cake:

153	Calories	3 %	Calories from Fat
2 g	Protein	1 g	Fiber
36 g	Carbohydrates	157 mg	Sodium
0 g	Fat	0 mg	Cholesterol

Sauce:

64	Calories	7 %	Calories from Fat
0 g	Protein	0 g	Fiber
14 g	Carbohydrates	5 mg	Sodium
0 g	Fat	0 mg	Cholesterol

Total:

217	Calories	2 %	Calories from Fat
2 g	Protein	1 g	Fiber
50 g	Carbohydrates	162 mg	Sodium
0 g	Fat	0 mg	Cholesterol

Strawberry and Kiwi Sorbet
in Cantaloupe Purée

A very light and refreshing dessert to serve with an assortment of lowfat cookies and cake.

8 servings

Basic Syrup
2 cups water
2 cups sugar

Strawberry Sorbet
1 quart strawberries
1 1/2 tablespoons fresh lemon juice
2/3 cup Basic Syrup

Kiwi Sorbet
6 kiwis, peeled
1 1/2 tablespoons fresh lemon juice
2/3 cup Basic Syrup

Cantaloupe Purée
2 cups cubed cantaloupe
1 tablespoon sugar
1 tablespoon Mandarine Napoléan liqueur or
    Grand Marnier (optional)

Mint sprigs for garnish

To make basic syrup: Combine water and sugar in a medium-size heavy saucepan over moderate heat and bring to a boil, stirring occasionally. Let simmer for 1 minute. Store syrup in refrigerator, covered, until ready to use. The syrup should be very cold before adding to the sorbets.

To make strawberry sorbet: In work bowl of food processor, purée the strawberries. Add lemon juice and cold syrup and blend until smooth. Pour strawberry mixture into ice cream maker and prepare according to manufacturer's directions. When ready, the sorbet can be served right away or kept in the freezer for one week. If frozen, it should be allowed to sit at room temperature for 15 to 20 minutes before serving.

To make kiwi sorbet: In work bowl of food processor, puree the kiwis. Add lemon juice and cold syrup and blend until smooth. Pour kiwi mixture into ice cream maker and prepare according to manufacturer's directions. When ready, the sorbet can be served right away or kept in the freezer for one week. If frozen, it should be allowed to sit at room temperature for 15 to 20 minutes before serving.

To make cantaloupe purée: In work bowl of food processor, puree cantaloupe and sugar until smooth. Pour cantaloupe into a strainer that has been placed over a large bowl. Push down on the cantaloupe to remove as much liquid as possible. Discard cantaloupe pulp and add liqueur to liquid and blend well.

When ready to serve: Spoon about 2 tablespoons cantaloupe purée into a serving dish. Top with 1 small scoop of strawberry sorbet and 1 scoop of kiwi sorbet. Garnish with a fresh sprig of mint.

Nutritional analysis per serving:

150	Calories	6 %	Calories from Fat
1 g	Protein	4 g	Fiber
37 g	Carbohydrates	8 mg	Sodium
1 g	Fat	0 mg	Cholesterol

Strawberry and White Chocolate Cake

This cake tastes like strawberries dipped in white chocolate! My favorite way to serve this dessert is to place eight dipped strawberries on the top edge of the cake, or serve each piece of cake with a dipped strawberry on the side.

16 servings

Cake
1 cup bread flour
6 tablespoons sugar
1 1/2 teaspoons baking powder
1/8 teaspoon salt
1/2 cup skim milk
1/2 teaspoon vanilla
1/4 cup applesauce
2 egg whites, at room temperature
2 tablespoons sugar

White Chocolate Mousse
6 ounces white chocolate, chopped
1 carton (8 ounces) frozen nondairy whip cream, thawed

1 cup sliced strawberries

Dipped Strawberries (optional)
4 ounces white chocolate, chopped
8 strawberries

Preheat oven to 350 degrees.

To make cake: Combine flour, 6 tablespoons sugar, baking powder, and salt in a large mixing bowl.

Combine milk, vanilla, and applesauce in a small bowl and blend well.

In mixing bowl of electric mixer, beat egg whites on moderate speed until foamy. Gradually add 2 tablespoons sugar and beat on high speed until stiff peaks form but are not dry. Add applesauce mixture to egg whites and beat on moderately low speed until just blended. Add applesauce and egg white mixture to dry ingredients and quickly mix with a fork to blend. Pour batter into an 8-inch round cake pan and bake for 20 to 25 minutes, or until cake tester inserted into center of cake comes out clean. Cover cake with waxed paper and cool on a cake rack for 10 minutes. Remove cake from pan, recover with waxed paper, and cool completely.

To make white chocolate mousse: Place 6 ounces white chocolate in small heavy saucepan, covered, over low heat. Cook just until chocolate is soft enough to blend; mix until smooth. Set aside for a few minutes.

In mixing bowl of electric mixer, beat whip cream until soft peaks form. Add melted white chocolate and beat on moderate speed until mixture is blended.

When ready to assemble cake: Using a serrated knife, cut cake in half horizontally to make two cake layers. Set first cake layer on an 8-inch cardboard round or cake plate. Place 3-inch strips of waxed paper under edges of cake (this will prevent frosting from getting on clean plate). Spread a thin layer of white chocolate mousse on cake layer and top with sliced strawberries; spread a thin layer of mousse over strawberries. Place second cake layer on top of strawberries and frost top and sides of cake with remaining white chocolate mousse. Remove waxed paper strips and refrigerate cake for several hours or overnight.

To make dipped strawberries: Melt 4 ounces white chocolate in a small heavy saucepan, covered, over low heat. Cook just until chocolate is soft enough to blend. Dip 8 strawberries into the melted chocolate, one at a time, leaving hull and top of strawberry undipped. Allow excess chocolate to drip into saucepan. Place each dipped strawberry on a piece of waxed paper to set. To decorate cake, place dipped strawberries around the top edge of cake.

Nutritional analysis per serving:

Cake:

60	Calories	1 %	Calories from Fat
2 g	Protein	0 g	Fiber
13 g	Carbohydrates	62 mg	Sodium
1 g	Fat	10 mg	Cholesterol

Mousse:

95	Calories	66 %	Calories from Fat
1 g	Protein	0 g	Fiber
8 g	Carbohydrates	20 mg	Sodium
7 g	Fat	2 mg	Cholesterol

Total with strawberries:

155	Calories	46 %	Calories from Fat
3 g	Protein	1 g	Fiber
21 g	Carbohydrates	82 mg	Sodium
8 g	Fat	2 mg	Cholesterol

Sugar-and-Spice Pumpkin Cupcakes

These spicy cupcakes are a welcome treat during Halloween. Serve them to your trick-or-treaters and wait for the rave reviews.

8 cupcakes

3/4 cup unbleached flour
2/3 cup firmly packed dark brown sugar
1 teaspoon cinnamon
1/2 teaspoon ginger
1/4 teaspoon *each* nutmeg and ground cloves
1/8 teaspoon allspice
1/4 teaspoon *each* baking powder and baking soda
1/8 teaspoon salt
1/2 cup raisins (optional)
1/2 cup prune lekvar
1 egg white
1/2 cup solid-pack canned pumpkin
1 teaspoon vanilla

Preheat oven to 350 degrees.

Combine flour, brown sugar, cinnamon, ginger, nutmeg, cloves, allspice, baking powder, baking soda, salt, and raisins in a large mixing bowl.

Combine lekvar, egg white, pumpkin, and vanilla in a small mixing bowl and blend well. Add pumpkin mixture to dry ingredients and mix with a fork until blended. Spoon batter two-thirds full into muffin cups that have been coated with vegetable spray. Bake for 25 minutes, or until golden brown. Remove cupcakes from pan, cover with waxed paper, and let cool. Store cupcakes in an airtight container.

Note: The cupcakes are delicious when iced with Cream Cheese Frosting (recipe is on page 213).

Nutritional analysis per cupcake:

184	Calories	2 %	Calories from Fat
2 g	Protein	3 g	Fiber
44 g	Carbohydrates	92 mg	Sodium
0 g	Fat	0 mg	Cholesterol

Sunshine Lemon Cake

The intense lemon flavor in this two-layered cake frosted with a luscious lemony frosting is sure to please lemon fans!

16 servings

Lemon Cake
2 cups bread flour
3/4 cup granulated sugar
1 tablespoon baking powder
1/4 teaspoon salt
1 jar (6 ounces) pear baby food
1 cup skim milk
1 teaspoon vanilla
1 tablespoon finely grated lemon peel
1/8 teaspoon lemon oil
4 egg whites, at room temperature
1/4 cup granulated sugar

Lemon Frosting
2 tablespoons *each* fat-free and light margarine, at
    room temperature
2 tablespoons fresh lemon juice
1 tablespoon finely grated lemon peel
3 cups powdered sugar

Preheat oven to 350 degrees.

To make lemon cake: Combine flour, 3/4 cup granulated sugar, baking powder, and salt in a large mixing bowl.

Combine pears, milk, vanilla, lemon peel, and lemon oil in a small bowl and blend well.

In mixing bowl of electric mixer, beat egg whites on moderate speed until they are foamy. Gradually add 1/4 cup granulated sugar, 1 tablespoon at a time, beating well after each addition. Increase speed to high and beat until stiff peaks form but are not dry. Add lemon mixture to egg whites and beat on moderate speed to lightly blend. Add lemon and egg white mixture to dry ingredients and quickly mix with a fork to blend. Pour batter into two 8-inch round cake pans that have been coated with vegetable spray. Bake for 25 minutes, or until cake tester inserted into center of cakes comes out clean. Cover cakes with waxed paper and cool on cake racks for 10 minutes. Remove cakes from pans, recover with waxed paper, and cool completely.

To make lemon frosting: In mixing bowl of electric mixer, beat margarines until smooth. Add lemon juice, lemon peel, and 2 cups of the powdered sugar and beat until blended. Add the remaining 1 cup powdered sugar and beat until light and fluffy.

To assemble cake: Set first cake layer on an 8-inch cardboard round or cake plate and place 3-inch strips of waxed paper under edges of cake (this will prevent frosting from getting on clean plate). Spread a thin layer of lemon frosting on first layer, top with second cake layer and spread remaining frosting on top and sides. Remove waxed paper strips and refrigerate cake for several hours.

Nutritional analysis per serving:

Cake:

124	Calories	2 %	Calories from Fat
3 g	Protein	0 g	Fiber
27 g	Carbohydrates	110 mg	Sodium
0 g	Fat	0 mg	Cholesterol

Frosting:

78	Calories	6 %	Calories from Fat
0 g	Protein	0 g	Fiber
19 g	Carbohydrates	18 mg	Sodium
1 g	Fat	0 mg	Cholesterol

Total:

202	Calories	4 %	Calories from Fat
3 g	Protein	0 g	Fiber
46 g	Carbohydrates	128 mg	Sodium
1 g	Fat	0 mg	Cholesterol

Whiskey Bread Pudding

This otherwise "homey" bread pudding is deliciously enhanced by a warm whiskey sauce.

16 servings

Bread Pudding
3 cups skim milk
3/4 cup granulated sugar
1/2 cup egg substitute
1 1/2 tablespoons vanilla
1 tablespoon pear baby food
4 cups cubed fat-free firm white or French bread
1/2 cup raisins

Whiskey Sauce
1/4 cup pear baby food
2 tablespoons light margarine
1 cup powdered sugar
1/4 cup egg substitute
1/4 cup whiskey

Preheat oven to 325 degrees.

To make bread pudding: Combine milk, granulated sugar, 1/2 cup egg substitute, vanilla, and 1 tablespoon pears in a large mixing bowl and blend well. Add bread cubes and raisins and blend well. Pour bread pudding into an 8 × 11.5 × 2-inch baking dish that has been coated with vegetable spray. Bake for 1 hour.

To make whiskey sauce: Twenty minutes before bread pudding is done, combine 1/4 cup pears, margarine, and powdered sugar in a small heavy saucepan over moderate heat and stir until the mixture is smooth and hot. Remove saucepan from heat and add 1/4 cup egg substitute and whiskey and quickly blend with a whisk until smooth. Spoon a generous amount of warm sauce over each serving of hot bread pudding.

Nutritional analysis per serving:

Pudding:

94	Calories	3 %	Calories from Fat
3 g	Protein	0 g	Fiber
20 g	Carbohydrates	67 mg	Sodium
0 g	Fat	1 mg	Cholesterol

Sauce:

39	Calories	18 %	Calories from Fat
0 g	Protein	0 g	Fiber
7 g	Carbohydrates	8 mg	Sodium
1 g	Fat	0 mg	Cholesterol

Total:

133	Calories	6 %	Calories from Fat
3 g	Protein	0 g	Fiber
27 g	Carbohydrates	75 mg	Sodium
1 g	Fat	1 mg	Cholesterol

Special Occasion Cakes

Black Forest Cake

Most recipes for Black Forest Cake include a cherry filling that is cooked and thickened. I prefer to make this cake with cherry preserves so there is only a hint of the cherry flavor, which accents the sweetness of the whipped cream and the intensity of the chocolate. This cake has a little more fat than some of the other desserts in the cookbook, but it is worth the indulgence.

12 servings

Cake
2 cups bread flour
1 cup sugar
1 tablespoon baking powder
1/8 teaspoon salt
2/3 cup buttermilk
1 egg
3 egg whites
1 jar (6 ounces) pear baby food
2 tablespoons canola oil
2 teaspoons vanilla

2 tablespoons Kirsch or cherry brandy
1 jar (8 ounces) good-quality cherry preserves

Whip Cream Frosting
1 carton (8 ounces) frozen nondairy whip cream, defrosted
 and whipped according to carton directions

1 container (3 1/2 ounces) chocolate sprinkles
Chocolate curls (page 274)
Powdered sugar (optional)

Preheat oven to 350 degrees.

To make cake: Combine flour, sugar, baking powder, and salt in a large mixing bowl.

Combine buttermilk, egg, egg whites, pears, oil, and vanilla in a small bowl and blend well. Add buttermilk mixture to dry ingredients and mix with a fork until blended. Pour batter into two 9-inch round cake pans that have been coated with vegetable spray. Bake for 20 to 25 minutes, or until cake tester inserted into center of cakes comes out clean. Cover cakes with waxed paper and cool on cake racks.

When ready to assemble cake: Place first cake layer on a 9-inch cardboard round or cake plate. Place 3-inch strips of waxed paper under edges of cake (this will prevent whipped cream from getting on clean plate). Brush cake layer with 1 tablespoon Kirsch and spread cherry preserves within 1/4-inch from edge of cake layer. Place second cake layer on top of first and brush with remaining Kirsch. Frost top and sides with whipped cream. Press chocolate sprinkles onto sides of cake and sprinkle chocolate curls over top. Remove and discard waxed paper strips.

Note: Before sprinkling chocolate curls over cake, reserve 1/2 cup whipped cream. Spoon into a pastry bag fitted with a star tip. Pipe rosettes around top edge of cake, then sprinkle top with chocolate curls. Dust with powdered sugar, if desired.

Nutritional analysis per serving:

Cake:

239	Calories	11 %	Calories from Fat
4 g	Protein	1 g	Fiber
49 g	Carbohydrates	404 mg	Sodium
3 g	Fat	18 mg	Cholesterol

Topping:

73	Calories	62 %	Calories from Fat
1g	Protein	0 g	Fiber
6 g	Carbohydrates	11 mg	Sodium
5 g	Fat	2 mg	Cholesterol

Total:

312	Calories	23 %	Calories from Fat
5 g	Protein	1 g	Fiber
55 g	Carbohydrates	415 mg	Sodium
8 g	Fat	20 mg	Cholesterol

Buttermilk Cake with
White Chocolate Glaze

This superb cake, cloaked in a satiny white chocolate glaze, can be enjoyed after a family dinner or dressed up for guests. I like to decorate the top with an apricot rose (page 274) or draw hearts into the white chocolate glaze.

12 servings

Buttermilk Cake
1 cup unbleached flour
$1/2$ cup sugar
$1/2$ tablespoon baking powder
$1/4$ teaspoon salt
$1/3$ cup buttermilk
1 egg
1 egg white
$1/4$ cup pear baby food
1 tablespoon canola oil
1 teaspoon vanilla

White Chocolate Glaze
2 tablespoons frozen nondairy whip cream, defrosted
1 teaspoon light corn syrup
6 ounces white chocolate, chopped

Preheat oven to 350 degrees.

To make buttermilk cake: Combine flour, sugar, baking powder, and salt in a large mixing bowl.

Combine buttermilk, egg, egg white, pears, oil, and vanilla in a small bowl and blend well. Add buttermilk mixture to dry ingredients and mix with a fork until blended. Spoon batter into a 9-inch round cake pan that has been coated with vegetable spray. Bake for 20 minutes, or until cake tester inserted into center of cake comes out clean. Cover cake with waxed paper and cool on cake rack for 10 minutes. Remove cake from pan, recover with waxed paper, and let cool completely.

To make white chocolate glaze: Place whip cream and corn syrup in a small heavy saucepan over moderate heat and bring to a boil, stirring occasionally. Remove saucepan from heat and add white chocolate; let chocolate sit for a couple of minutes. Stir until chocolate is well blended. Let the glaze sit for 10 to 15 minutes, or until thick enough to spread.

When ready to assemble cake: Set cake on a 9-inch cardboard round or cake plate. Place 3-inch strips of waxed paper under edges of cake (this will prevent glaze from getting on clean plate). Spread glaze over top and sides of cake; remove and discard waxed paper strips.

Nutritional analysis per serving:

Cake:

85	Calories	11 %	Calories from Fat
2 g	Protein	0 g	Fiber
17 g	Carbohydrates	230 mg	Sodium
1 g	Fat	18 mg	Cholesterol

Glaze:

85	Calories	53 %	Calories from Fat
1g	Protein	0 g	Fiber
9 g	Carbohydrates	2 mg	Sodium
5 g	Fat	0 mg	Cholesterol

Total:

170	Calories	32 %	Calories from Fat
3 g	Protein	1 g	Fiber
26 g	Carbohydrates	108 mg	Sodium
6 g	Fat	3 mg	Cholesterol

Carrot Cake

My favorite recipe for carrot cake calls for 1 1/2 cups oil. When I made the cake with only 2 tablespoons oil and 1/2 cup prune lekvar, I was amazed at how exceptionally moist and delicious the cake remained with no appreciable change in texture or flavor. I like to place miniature marzipan carrots around the top edge or in the center of the cake for a special touch.

16 servings

Carrot Cake
2 1/2 cups unbleached flour
1 1/4 cups granulated sugar
2 teaspoons cinnamon
2 teaspoons baking powder
1 1/2 teaspoons baking soda
1/4 teaspoon salt
6 carrots, cut into 2-inch chunks
1/2 cup prune lekvar
3 tablespoons pear baby food
2 tablespoons canola oil
1 egg
3 egg whites
1 can (8 ounces) unsweetened crushed pineapple, drained

Cream Cheese Frosting
6 ounces Neufchâtel or light cream cheese, at
   room temperature
1 1/2 cups powdered sugar
1 teaspoon vanilla

Preheat oven to 350 degrees.

To make carrot cake: Combine flour, granulated sugar, cinnamon, baking powder, baking soda, and salt in a large mixing bowl.

Place carrots in work bowl of food processor and process until finely chopped. Add lekvar, pears, oil, egg, egg whites, and pineapple and process until smooth. Add carrot mixture to dry ingredients and mix with a fork until blended. Spoon batter evenly into two 9-inch round cake pans that have been coated with vegetable spray. Bake for 30 to 35 minutes, or until cake tester inserted into center of cakes comes out clean. Cover cakes with waxed paper and cool on cake racks for 10 minutes. Remove cakes from pans, recover with waxed paper, and cool completely.

To make cream cheese frosting: Combine cream cheese, powdered sugar, and vanilla in bowl of electric mixer. Beat until smooth.

When ready to assemble cake: Set first cake layer on a cake plate and spread half of the frosting on top of cake. Top with second cake layer and spread remaining frosting on top only. Refrigerate cake for several hours. When ready to serve, bring cake to room temperature.

Nutritional analysis per serving:

Cake:

199	Calories	9 %	Calories from Fat
3 g	Protein	2 g	Fiber
42 g	Carbohydrates	177 mg	Sodium
2 g	Fat	13 mg	Cholesterol

Frosting:

65	Calories	42 %	Calories from Fat
1 g	Protein	0 g	Fiber
10 g	Carbohydrates	42 mg	Sodium
3 g	Fat	8 mg	Cholesterol

Total:

264	Calories	17 %	Calories from Fat
4 g	Protein	2 g	Fiber
52 g	Carbohydrates	219 mg	Sodium
5 g	Fat	21 mg	Cholesterol

Celebration Chocolate Cake

The intensity of the chocolate and the sweetness of the raspberries harmonize perfectly, resulting in the ultimate dessert. This is one of my favorite desserts for dinner parties because it can be made so dramatic in appearance simply topped with a white chocolate rose or bow (page 275) or adorned with 12 fresh raspberries and small fresh mint leaves placed around the top edge of the cake.

12 servings

Chocolate Cake
1 cup unbleached flour
1 cup sugar
1 can (16 ounces) chocolate syrup
1/2 cup prune lekvar
4 egg whites
1 teaspoon almond extract
1/4 cup good-quality raspberry preserves

Chocolate Glaze
5 ounces chocolate chips
3 tablespoons liquid nondairy creamer

Preheat oven to 350 degrees.

To make chocolate cake: Coat a 9-inch round cake pan with vegetable spray, line with waxed paper, and coat again with vegetable spray. Flour pan and shake out excess. Set aside.

Combine flour and sugar in a large mixing bowl.

Combine chocolate syrup, lekvar, egg whites, and almond extract in a medium-size bowl; blend well. Add chocolate mixture to dry ingredients and mix with a fork until blended.

Pour batter evenly into cake pan and bake for 45 to 50 minutes, or until cake tester inserted into center of cake comes out clean. Cover cake with waxed paper and cool on a cake rack. When cake is cool, remove from pan and paper. Place cake on a 9-inch cardboard round and set it on a cake rack placed over a large piece of waxed paper. Spread raspberry preserves over top of cake and set aside.

To make chocolate glaze: Place chocolate chips and nondairy creamer in a small heavy saucepan, covered, over low heat. Cook just until chocolate is soft enough to blend. Remove glaze from heat, blend well, and let sit 15 to 20 minutes, or until thick enough to spread.

When ready to glaze cake: Spread chocolate glaze over top and sides of cake. The glaze on the sides may drip onto the waxed paper; occasionally smooth sides until the frosting is firm. Store cake in an airtight container.

Nutritional analysis per serving:

Cake:

244	Calories	2 %	Calories from Fat
3 g	Protein	2 g	Fiber
58 g	Carbohydrates	62 mg	Sodium
0 g	Fat	0 mg	Cholesterol

Frosting:

73	Calories	62 %	Calories from Fat
0 g	Protein	0 g	Fiber
7 g	Carbohydrates	4 mg	Sodium
5 g	Fat	0 mg	Cholesterol

Total:

317	Calories	14 %	Calories from Fat
3 g	Protein	2 g	Fiber
65 g	Carbohydrates	66 mg	Sodium
5 g	Fat	0 mg	Cholesterol

Special Occasion Cakes

Chocolate Apricot Torte

For a striking effect, set three apricot roses (page 274) on top of the cake.

12 servings

Chocolate Cake
1/2 cup Dutch process cocoa
2/3 cup unbleached flour
1/2 cup sugar
2 tablespoons finely ground walnuts
1 teaspoon baking powder
1/8 teaspoon salt
1/2 cup apricot butter (see Helpful Hints)
2 egg whites
1/2 cup egg substitute
2 tablespoons coffee liqueur

Chocolate Glaze
4 tablespoons Dutch process cocoa
2 tablespoons liquid nondairy creamer
2 tablespoons light corn syrup
1 tablespoon sugar
2 teaspoons vanilla
1 teaspoon honey

1/4 cup good-quality apricot preserves (for glaze)

Preheat oven to 375 degrees.

To make chocolate cake: Coat an 8-inch cake pan with vegetable spray and lightly dust with flour. Set aside.

Combine cocoa, flour, sugar, walnuts, baking powder, and salt in a large mixing bowl.

Combine apricot, egg whites, egg substitute, and coffee liqueur in a small bowl and blend well. Combine apricot mixture with dry ingredients and mix with a fork until blended. Pour batter into prepared pan and bake for 30 to 35 minutes, or until cake tester inserted into center of cake comes out clean. Cover cake with waxed paper and cool on cake rack.

To make chocolate glaze: Combine cocoa, nondairy creamer, corn syrup, sugar, vanilla, and honey in a small saucepan over moderately low heat. Bring to a boil, stirring occasionally. Let glaze sit for 10 to 15 minutes, or until thick enough to spread.

When ready to assemble torte: Remove cake from pan and set on an 8-inch cardboard round, then on a cake rack placed over a large piece of waxed paper. Pour glaze over cake, allowing it to run down sides. With a spatula, scrape up chocolate that has dripped onto the waxed paper and spread it on top and sides of cake. Refrigerate cake until glaze is firm, about 20 minutes.

After cake has chilled for about 20 minutes, make the apricot glaze. Place apricot preserves in small saucepan and bring to a boil over moderate heat, stirring occasionally. Place cooked apricot in a sieve set over a bowl and press down with the back of a spoon to extract as much liquid as possible; discard pulp. Quickly spread apricot liquid over top of cake. Refrigerate cake for several hours or overnight. Bring to room temperature before serving.

Nutritional analysis per serving:

Cake:

102	Calories	18 %	Calories from Fat
3 g	Protein	2 g	Fiber
18 g	Carbohydrates	95 mg	Sodium
2 g	Fat	0 mg	Cholesterol

Glaze:

49	Calories	19 %	Calories from Fat
0 g	Protein	1 g	Fiber
9 g	Carbohydrates	17 mg	Sodium
1 g	Fat	0 mg	Cholesterol

Total:

143	Calories	17 %	Calories from Fat
3 g	Protein	2 g	Fiber
28 g	Carbohydrates	112 mg	Sodium
3 g	Fat	0 mg	Cholesterol

Chocolate Cloud Cake

This recipe was featured in a Los Angeles Times *article on baking without fat* .

12 servings

Chocolate Cake
2 cups flour
1 cup unsweetened cocoa
2 cups granulated sugar
2 teaspoons baking soda
1 teaspoon baking powder
1/4 teaspoon salt
4 jars (2 1/2 ounces each) prune baby food
2 teaspoons vanilla
2 eggs, beaten
1 cup nonfat milk
2 tablespoons instant espresso coffee powder
1 cup boiling water

Seven-Minute Frosting (optional)
1 tablespoon instant espresso coffee powder
1/4 cup hot water
3 egg whites
1 1/2 cups firmly packed light brown sugar
1 teaspoon cream of tartar
1 teaspoon vanilla

Preheat oven to 350 degrees.

To make chocolate cake: Sift together flour, cocoa, granulated sugar, baking soda, baking powder, and salt into mixing bowl. Stir until blended. Add prunes, vanilla, eggs, and milk and stir just until blended.

Special Occasion Cakes

Combine espresso and boiling water and stir until dissolved. Stir into batter until blended. Pour batter into two 9-inch round cake pans sprayed with vegetable spray. Bake for 30 to 35 minutes, or until cake tester inserted into center of cakes comes out clean. Let cakes cool in pans 10 minutes. Invert onto racks to cool.

To make seven-minute frosting: Dissolve coffee in hot water. Combine egg whites, brown sugar, coffee mixture, and cream of tartar in top of double boiler. Beat with mixer until frosting forms stiff peaks, 5 to 7 minutes. Remove from heat. Add vanilla. Makes about 5 cups.

When ready to assemble cake: Spread top of first layer with frosting. Top with second layer and frost top and sides.

Nutritional analysis per serving:

Cake:

257	Calories	7 %	Calories from Fat
6 g	Protein	0 g	Fiber
58 g	Carbohydrates	161 mg	Sodium
2 g	Fat	36 mg	Cholesterol

Frosting:

72	Calories	0 %	Calories from Fat
1 g	Protein	0 g	Fiber
18 g	Carbohydrates	35 mg	Sodium
0 g	Fat	0 mg	Cholesterol

Total:

329	Calories	5 %	Calories from Fat
7 g	Protein	0 g	Fiber
76 g	Carbohydrates	196 mg	Sodium
2 g	Fat	36 mg	Cholesterol

Chocolate Gateau

This cake will serve perfectly as the crowning finale to an intimate dinner party. It is exceptionally rich and moist and almost tastes like a truffle. I like to decorate the cake with a gold ribbon tied around it.

6 servings

Chocolate Cake
2 ounces unsweetened chocolate, chopped
2 ounces semisweet chocolate, chopped
1/3 cup sugar
1/4 cup unbleached flour
1/8 teaspoon salt
1/2 cup prune lekvar
4 egg whites
1 teaspoon vanilla

Chocolate Glaze
1/2 cup chocolate chips
2 tablespoons liquid nondairy creamer
2 teaspoons sugar

Preheat oven to 350 degrees.

To make chocolate cake: Place chocolates in a small heavy saucepan, covered, over low heat. Cook just until chocolate softens; stir until smooth. Set aside.

Combine 1/3 cup sugar, flour, and salt in a large mixing bowl.

Combine lekvar, egg whites, vanilla, and chocolate in a small bowl and blend well. Add chocolate mixture to dry ingredients and mix with a fork until blended. Spoon batter into an 8-inch springform pan or cake pan that has been coated with vegetable spray. Bake for 30 minutes, or until cake tester inserted into center of cake comes out clean. Cover cake with waxed paper and cool on a cake rack.

To make chocolate glaze: Place chocolate chips, nondairy creamer, and sugar in a small heavy saucepan over low heat. Cook just until chocolate begins to soften. Remove pan from heat and blend mixture until smooth.

When ready to assemble cake: Remove cake from pan and set on a cake rack placed over a large piece of waxed paper. Immediately spread glaze on top and sides of cooled cake. Store cake in an airtight container.

Nutritional analysis per serving:

Cake:

236	Calories	31 %	Calories from Fat
4 g	Protein	3 g	Fiber
37 g	Carbohydrates	95 mg	Sodium
8 g	Fat	0 mg	Cholesterol

Glaze:

98	Calories	55 %	Calories from Fat
1 g	Protein	0 g	Fiber
10 g	Carbohydrates	6 mg	Sodium
6 g	Fat	0 mg	Cholesterol

Total:

334	Calories	38 %	Calories from Fat
5 g	Protein	3 g	Fiber
47 g	Carbohydrates	101 mg	Sodium
14 g	Fat	0 mg	Cholesterol

Chocolate Hazelnut Torte

The terms hazelnuts and filberts are often used interchangeably; however, filberts are actually cultivated hazelnuts. When the toasted hazelnuts are baked in this cake, their dominant flavor enhances the flavors of the chocolate and prune lekvar.

12 servings

Chocolate Hazelnut Cake
3/4 cup chocolate chips
1/3 cup unbleached flour
1/2 cup sugar
2 tablespoons finely ground toasted hazelnuts
Pinch of salt
1/2 cup prune lekvar
3 egg whites
2 tablespoons Grand Marnier

Chocolate Glaze
1/2 cup chocolate chips
1 1/2 tablespoons liquid nondairy creamer
1 teaspoon light corn syrup

Caramelized hazelnuts (optional)

Preheat oven to 375 degrees.

To make chocolate hazelnut cake: Coat an 8-inch springform pan with vegetable spray, line bottom with waxed paper, and spray again. Dust lightly with flour.

Place chocolate chips in a small heavy saucepan, covered, over low heat. Cook until chocolate is soft enough to blend. Set aside.

Combine flour, sugar, hazelnuts, and salt in a large mixing bowl.

Combine lekvar, egg whites, Grand Marnier, and chocolate in a small bowl and blend well.

Add lekvar mixture to dry ingredients and mix with a fork until blended. Spoon batter into prepared pan and bake for 30 to 35 minutes, or until cake tester inserted into center of cake comes out clean. Cover cake with waxed paper and cool on cake rack. Remove cake from pan and ice with chocolate glaze.

To make chocolate glaze: Combine chocolate chips, cream, and corn syrup in a small heavy saucepan, covered, over low heat. Cook just until chocolate is soft enough to blend. Remove saucepan from heat and blend mixture until smooth. Let chocolate sit for 5 minutes, or until thick enough to spread.

When ready to assemble cake: Set cake on an 8-inch cardboard round or cake plate. Place 3-inch strips of waxed paper under edges of cake (this will prevent glaze from getting on clean plate). Spread glaze over top and sides of cake. When glaze has set, remove waxed paper strips and store cake in an airtight container. For an added touch, place caramelized hazelnuts around top edge of cake if desired. See recipe on page 276.

Nutritional analysis per serving:

Cake:

166	Calories	33 %	Calories from Fat
2 g	Protein	1 g	Fiber
26 g	Carbohydrates	44 mg	Sodium
6 g	Fat	0 mg	Cholesterol

Glaze:

47	Calories	57 %	Calories from Fat
0 g	Protein	0 g	Fiber
5 g	Carbohydrates	3 mg	Sodium
3 g	Fat	0 mg	Cholesterol

Total:

213	Calories	33 %	Calories from Fat
2 g	Protein	2 g	Fiber
31 g	Carbohydrates	47 mg	Sodium
9 g	Fat	0 mg	Cholesterol

Devil's Food Cake

Birthdays and holidays are occasions that call for a special cake. This one consists of two rich, dense chocolate layers filled and frosted with a subtle chocolate whip cream. The cake is spectacular when topped with a dark chocolate rose (page 275) or when chocolate sprinkles are pressed onto its sides and rosettes are piped on the top edge.

12 servings

Devil's Food Cake
1 1/2 cups unbleached flour
1 cup sugar
1 1/2 teaspoons baking powder
1 teaspoon baking soda
1/4 teaspoon salt
2 heaping tablespoons Dutch process cocoa
1 jar (2 1/2 ounces) prune baby food
1/2 cup buttermilk
3 egg whites
2 teaspoons vanilla

Chocolate Whip-Cream Frosting
1 carton (8 ounces) frozen nondairy whip cream, defrosted
2 tablespoons Dutch process cocoa

Preheat oven to 350 degrees.

To make devil's food cake: Combine flour, sugar, baking powder, baking soda, salt, and cocoa in a large mixing bowl.

Combine prunes, buttermilk, egg whites, and vanilla in a small bowl and blend well. Add prune mixture to dry ingredients and mix with a fork until blended. Spoon batter into two 8-inch round cake pans that have been coated with vegetable spray and bake for 20 minutes, or until cake tester inserted into center of cake comes out clean. Cover cakes with waxed paper and cool on cake racks.

To make chocolate whip-cream frosting: Place whip cream and cocoa in mixing bowl of electric mixer and beat until light and fluffy.

When ready to assemble cake: Set first cake layer on an 8-inch cardboard round or cake plate. Place 3-inch strips of waxed paper under edges of cake (this will prevent whipped cream from getting on clean plate). Spread a thick layer of whipped cream on first layer, top with second cake layer and spread remaining whipped cream on top and sides. Remove waxed paper strips and refrigerate cake for several hours.

Nutritional analysis per serving:

Cake:

145	Calories	6 %	Calories from Fat
4 g	Protein	2 g	Fiber
30 g	Carbohydrates	182 mg	Sodium
1 g	Fat	0 mg	Cholesterol

Glaze:

35	Calories	77 %	Calories from Fat
0 g	Protein	0 g	Fiber
2 g	Carbohydrates	13 mg	Sodium
3 g	Fat	0 mg	Cholesterol

Total:

180	Calories	20 %	Calories from Fat
4 g	Protein	2 g	Fiber
32 g	Carbohydrates	195 mg	Sodium
4 g	Fat	0 mg	Cholesterol

German's Sweet Chocolate Cake

This classic chocolate cake is especially delicious when served on a bed of raspberry sauce or with the sauce and a few fresh raspberries spooned over the top.

8 servings

Chocolate Cake
5 ounces German's Sweet chocolate, chopped
1/4 cup flour
3/4 cup sugar
2 tablespoons finely chopped almonds
pinch of salt
1/2 cup prune lekvar
4 egg whites

Chocolate Glaze
3 ounces German's Sweet chocolate, chopped
1/2 teaspoon powdered instant coffee
1 tablespoon water

Raspberry Sauce
1 box (10 ounces) frozen raspberries in light syrup, defrosted
1/2 tablespoon sugar

white chocolate rose (optional)

Preheat oven to 375 degrees.

To make chocolate cake: Place chocolate in a small heavy saucepan, covered, over low heat. Cook just until chocolate is soft enough to blend. Set aside.

Combine flour, sugar, almonds, and salt in a medium-size mixing bowl.

Combine lekvar, egg whites, and melted chocolate in a small bowl and blend well. Add chocolate mixture to dry ingredients and mix with a fork until blended. Spoon batter into an 8-inch round cake pan that has been coated with vegetable spray and dusted with flour. Bake for 30 minutes, or until cake tester inserted into center of cake comes out clean. Cover cake with waxed paper and cool on a cake rack. When cake is cool, remove from pan and recover with waxed paper while preparing the chocolate glaze.

To make chocolate glaze: Combine chocolate, coffee, and water in a small heavy saucepan, covered, over low heat. Cook just until chocolate is soft enough to blend. Let chocolate sit until firm enough to spread.

To make raspberry sauce: Place raspberries and sugar in work bowl of food processor and process until smooth. Place raspberry purée in small saucepan and bring to a boil over medium-low heat, stirring frequently. Using the back of a large spoon, press the raspberry purée through a fine-meshed sieve that has been placed over a bowl. Discard seeds and refrigerate sauce.

When ready to assemble cake: Set cake on an 8-inch cardboard round or cake plate and place 3-inch strips of waxed paper under edges of cake (this will prevent glaze from getting on clean plate). Spread glaze on top and sides of cake, smoothing sides occasionally, until chocolate is firm. Remove waxed paper strips and refrigerate cake for several hours. Bring cake to room temperature before serving.

When ready to serve, spoon about 2 tablespoons raspberry sauce on each plate and place a slice of cake on the sauce.

Note: This cake looks beautiful when topped with a white chocolate rose (page 275). Place rose on cake while glaze is still wet.

Nutritional analysis per serving:

Cake:

243	Calories	26 %	Calories from Fat
3g	Protein	2 g	Fiber
42 g	Carbohydrates	73 mg	Sodium
7 g	Fat	0 mg	Cholesterol

Glaze:

60	Calories	60 %	Calories from Fat
0 g	Protein	0 g	Fiber
6 g	Carbohydrates	2 mg	Sodium
4 g	Fat	0 mg	Cholesterol

Sauce:

40	Calories	0 %	Calories from Fat
0 g	Protein	0 g	Fiber
10 g	Carbohydrates	0 mg	Sodium
0 g	Fat	0 mg	Cholesterol

Total:

343	Calories	29 %	Calories from Fat
3 g	Protein	4 g	Fiber
58 g	Carbohydrates	75 mg	Sodium
11 g	Fat	0 mg	Cholesterol

Mocha Walnut Torte

This is one of my signature desserts: a layer of chocolate cake made with walnuts and veiled with a silky milk chocolate glaze.

12 servings

Walnut Cake
3/4 cup chocolate chips
1/2 cup finely chopped walnuts
1/4 cup unbleached flour
1/2 cup sugar
1/2 cup prune lekvar
4 egg whites
1 teaspoon vanilla

Mocha Glaze
5 ounces milk chocolate, chopped
1 1/2 tablespoons liquid nondairy creamer
1 teaspoon powdered instant coffee

12 chocolate-covered coffee beans (optional)

Preheat oven to 350 degrees.

To make walnut cake: Coat an 8-inch round cake pan with vegetable spray, line bottom with waxed paper, and spray again. Dust lightly with flour.

Place chocolate chips in a small heavy saucepan, covered, over low heat. Cook until chocolate is soft enough to blend. Remove saucepan from heat and set aside.

Combine walnuts, flour, and sugar in a medium-size mixing bowl.

Combine lekvar, egg whites, vanilla, and melted chocolate in a small bowl and blend well.

Add chocolate mixture to dry ingredients and mix with a fork until blended. Spoon batter into prepared cake pan and bake for 45 to 50 minutes, or until cake tester inserted into center of cake comes out clean. Cover cake with waxed paper and cool on a cake rack.

To make mocha glaze: Place chocolate, creamer, and coffee in a small heavy saucepan, covered, over low heat. Cook until chocolate is soft enough to blend; mix until smooth.

When ready to assemble cake: Set cake on an 8-inch cardboard round or cake plate and place 3-inch strips of waxed paper under edges of cake (this will prevent glaze from getting on clean plate). Spread mocha glaze on top and sides of cake. Remove waxed paper strips and discard.

To decorate cake: Reserve 1/4 cup glaze and spoon it into a small pastry bag fitted with a small star tip. Pipe 12 rosettes, equally spaced, around top edge of cake. Place a coffee bean on each rosette.

Nutritional analysis per serving:

Cake:

171	Calories	37 %	Calories from Fat
3 g	Protein	2 g	Fiber
24 g	Carbohydrates	27 mg	Sodium
7 g	Fat	0 mg	Cholesterol

Glaze:

10	Calories	27 %	Calories from Fat
0 g	Protein	0 g	Fiber
2 g	Carbohydrates	9 mg	Sodium
1 g	Fat	0 mg	Cholesterol

Total:

181	Calories	35 %	Calories from Fat
3 g	Protein	2 g	Fiber
26 g	Carbohydrates	40 mg	Sodium
7 g	Fat	0 mg	Cholesterol

Regal Chocolate Torte

This very rich and dense chocolate cake is covered with a smooth chocolate glaze. I like to draw a white chocolate cobweb (page 276) on the glaze or top it with a fresh flower.

12 servings

Chocolate Cake
7 ounces semisweet chocolate, chopped
2/3 cup unbleached flour
1/2 cup sugar
2 tablespoons finely ground almonds
1 teaspoon baking powder
pinch of salt
1/2 cup prune lekvar
4 egg whites
2 tablespoons coffee liqueur
scant 1/8 teaspoon almond extract

Chocolate Glaze
4 ounces chocolate chips
3 tablespoons liquid nondairy creamer
1 tablespoon corn syrup

2 ounces white chocolate (optional)

Preheat oven to 375 degrees.

To make chocolate cake: Coat an 8-inch round cake pan with vegetable spray, line bottom with waxed paper, and spray again. Dust lightly with flour. Set aside.

   Place chocolate in medium-size saucepan, covered, and cook over low heat just until chocolate is soft enough to blend. Set aside.

Combine flour, sugar, almonds, baking powder, and salt in a large mixing bowl.

Combine lekvar, egg whites, coffee liqueur, and almond extract in a small bowl and blend well. Combine lekvar mixture with dry ingredients and mix with a fork to blend. Pour batter into prepared pan and bake for 30 to 35 minutes, or until cake tester inserted into center of cake comes out clean. Cover cake with waxed paper and cool on a cake rack.

To make chocolate glaze: Combine chocolate chips, creamer, and corn syrup in a heavy medium-size saucepan, covered, over low heat. Cook just until chocolate is soft enough to blend. Remove saucepan from heat and blend mixture until smooth. Let sit for 20 to 25 minutes, or until glaze is thick enough to spread.

To assemble cake: Remove cake from pan and discard waxed paper and set cake on a cake rack placed over a large piece of waxed paper. Spread glaze over top and sides of cake, scraping up the chocolate that has dripped onto the paper and respreading it on the cake. Refrigerate cake. Every 10 minutes, smooth glaze on the sides of the cake until it is firm. Once glaze is set, refrigerate cake for several hours. Bring cake to room temperature before serving.

Note: For a dramatic presentation, draw a white chocolate cobweb on the chocolate glaze before it has set. See recipe on page 276.

Nutritional analysis per serving:

Cake:

203	Calories	31 %	Calories from Fat
3 g	Protein	2 g	Fiber
32 g	Carbohydrates	77 mg	Sodium
7 g	Fat	0 mg	Cholesterol

Glaze:

102	Calories	53 %	Calories from Fat
1 g	Protein	1 g	Fiber
11 g	Carbohydrates	10 mg	Sodium
6 g	Fat	1 mg	Cholesterol

Total:

305	Calories	38 %	Calories from Fat
4 g	Protein	3 g	Fiber
43 g	Carbohydrates	87 mg	Sodium
13 g	Fat	1 mg	Cholesterol

Sachertorte

Sachertorte is a world-renowned dessert created in 1832 by the Viennese master cook Eduard Sacher. It is an exceptionally dense chocolate cake, sweetened with a layer of apricot preserves, and cloaked in a velvety chocolate glaze.

12 servings

Cake
5 ounces semisweet chocolate, chopped
1 cup unbleached flour
1/2 cup sugar
2 teaspoons baking powder
1/4 teaspoon salt
1/2 cup prune lekvar
6 egg whites
1 tablespoon vanilla

Apricot Glaze
1/2 cup good-quality apricot preserves

Chocolate Glaze
3/4 cup chocolate chips
3 scant tablespoons liquid nondairy creamer
1 tablespoon light corn syrup

1 to 2 ounces milk chocolate, melted (optional)

Preheat oven to 350 degrees.

To make chocolate cake: Coat a 9-inch springform pan with vegetable spray, line bottom with waxed paper, and spray again. Dust lightly with flour. Set aside.

Place chocolate in a small heavy saucepan, covered, over low heat. Cook until chocolate is soft enough to blend. Remove saucepan from heat and set aside.

Combine flour, sugar, baking powder, and salt in a large mixing bowl.

Combine lekvar, egg whites, vanilla, and melted chocolate in a small bowl and blend well. Add lekvar mixture to dry ingredients and mix with a fork until blended. Pour batter into prepared pan and bake for 35 to 40 minutes, or until cake tester inserted into center of cake comes out clean. Cover cake with waxed paper and cool on a cake rack for 15 minutes. Remove cake from pan and peel off waxed paper on bottom of cake. Recover cake with waxed paper and let cool completely.

To make apricot glaze: Place apricot preserves in a small heavy saucepan over moderate heat; bring just to a boil. Pour preserves into a fine-meshed sieve that has been placed over a small bowl. Press with the back of a spoon to remove as much liquid as possible; discard pulp. Remove waxed paper from cooled cake and spread apricot glaze over the top. Set aside.

To make chocolate glaze: Combine chocolate chips, creamer, and corn syrup in a small heavy saucepan, covered, over low heat. Cook just until chocolate is soft enough to blend. Remove saucepan from heat and blend mixture until smooth. Set aside for 5 to 10 minutes, or until glaze is thick enough to spread over top and sides of cake.

When ready to assemble cake: Place cake on a 9-inch cardboard round or cake plate and place 3-inch strips of waxed paper under edges of cake (this will prevent glaze from getting on clean plate). Spread glaze over top and sides of cake, smoothing the sides. Remove waxed paper strips and store cake in an airtight container.

To decorate cake (optional): Spoon milk chocolate into a small pastry bag fitted with a small writing tip and write the word *Sacher* across the top of the cake.

Note: For Passover, I substitute 1 cup matzoh cake meal for the flour and reduce the baking time by about 5 minutes.

Nutritional analysis per serving:

Cake with preserves:

204	Calories	18 %	Calories from Fat
3 g	Protein	1 g	Fiber
39 g	Carbohydrates	114 mg	Sodium
4 g	Fat	0 mg	Cholesterol

Glaze:

77	Calories	58 %	Calories from Fat
0 g	Protein	0 g	Fiber
8 g	Carbohydrates	5 mg	Sodium
5 g	Fat	0 mg	Cholesterol

Total:

281	Calories	29 %	Calories from Fat
3 g	Protein	2 g	Fiber
47 g	Carbohydrates	119 mg	Sodium
9 g	Fat	0 mg	Cholesterol

Sensational Chocolate Torte

This is a classic European style torte: two layers of fabulously rich chocolate cake, separated by a layer of apricot preserves, all encased in a silky chocolate glaze. The cake is gorgeous when topped with three apricot roses (page 274) or one large white chocolate rose (page 275).

12 servings

Chocolate Cake
2 ounces unsweetened chocolate, chopped
1/2 cup strong coffee
1 cup unbleached flour
1 cup sugar
1 teaspoon baking soda
1/4 teaspoon salt
3 tablespoons prune lekvar
1/4 cup buttermilk
1 egg white
1 teaspoon vanilla

6 tablespoons apricot preserves

Chocolate Glaze
1 cup chocolate chips
1/3 cup liquid nondairy creamer
1 tablespoon light corn syrup

Preheat oven to 350 degrees.

To make chocolate cake: Combine chocolate and coffee in a small heavy saucepan, covered, over moderately low heat. Cook just until chocolate is soft enough to blend. Set aside.

Combine flour, sugar, baking soda, and salt in a large mixing bowl.

Combine lekvar, buttermilk, egg white, vanilla, and chocolate in a medium-size bowl and blend well. Add chocolate mixture to dry ingredients and mix with a fork until blended. Spoon batter into two 8-inch round cake pans that have been coated with vegetable spray and dusted with flour. Bake for 20 to 25 minutes, or until cake tester inserted into center of cakes comes out clean. Cover cakes with waxed paper and cool on cake racks for 15 minutes. Remove cakes from pans, recover with waxed paper, and cool completely.

To make chocolate glaze: Combine chocolate chips, creamer, and corn syrup in a small heavy saucepan, covered, over moderately low heat. Cook just until chocolate is soft enough to blend. Remove saucepan from heat and blend mixture until smooth. Let glaze sit for 15 to 30 minutes, or until thick enough to spread.

When ready to assemble cake: Set first cake layer on an 8-inch cardboard round or cake plate and place 3-inch strips of waxed paper under edges of cake (this will prevent glaze from getting on clean plate). Spread apricot preserves on cake, leaving a 1/8-inch border all around the cake. Place the second cake layer on top of the first and spread chocolate glaze over top and sides of cake, smoothing sides occasionally. Remove waxed paper strips and refrigerate cake for several hours. Bring cake to room temperature before serving.

Nutritional analysis per serving:

Cake:

174	Calories	10 %	Calories from Fat
2 g	Protein	1 g	Fiber
37 g	Carbohydrates	127 mg	Sodium
2 g	Fat	0 mg	Cholesterol

Special Occasion Cakes

Glaze:

115	Calories	55 %	Calories from Fat
1 g	Protein	1 g	Fiber
12 g	Carbohydrates	9 mg	Sodium
7 g	Fat	0 mg	Cholesterol

Total:

289	Calories	28 %	Calories from Fat
3 g	Protein	1 g	Fiber
49 g	Carbohydrates	136 mg	Sodium
9 g	Fat	0 mg	Cholesterol

Special Occasion Cakes

Viennese Chocolate Torte

This European cake has an incredibly smooth texture and a heavenly chocolate essence. For a dramatic appearance, draw a white chocolate cobweb (page 276) on the chocolate glaze. Because this torte is higher in fat than many of the other desserts in this book, reserve it for those special occasions when an indulgence is in order.

12 servings

Chocolate Cake
6 ounces semisweet chocolate, chopped
1 1/3 cups almonds, finely chopped
3/4 cup sugar
1/8 teaspoon salt
1/2 cup prune lekvar
6 egg whites
1 teaspoon vanilla

Chocolate Glaze
5 ounces semisweet chocolate
1/4 cup liquid nondairy creamer
1 teaspoon powdered instant coffee

Preheat oven to 375 degrees.

To make chocolate cake: Place chocolate in a small heavy saucepan, covered, over low heat. Cook just until chocolate softens. Blend well. Set aside.

Combine almonds, sugar, and salt in a large mixing bowl.

Combine lekvar, egg whites, vanilla, and melted chocolate in a small bowl and blend well. Add chocolate mixture to dry ingredients and mix with a fork until blended. Spoon batter into an 8-inch springform pan that has been coated with vegetable spray. Bake for 35 to 40 minutes, or until cake tester inserted into center of cake comes out clean. Cover cake with waxed paper and cool on a cake rack.

To make chocolate glaze: Combine chocolate, creamer, and coffee in a small heavy saucepan, covered, over low heat. Cook just until chocolate softens; blend until smooth.

When ready to assemble cake: Set cake on an 8-inch cardboard round or cake plate and place 3-inch strips of waxed paper under edges of cake (this will prevent glaze from getting on clean plate). Spread glaze over top and sides of cake, smoothing the sides. Remove waxed paper strips and refrigerate cake for several hours or overnight. Bring the cake to room temperature before serving.

Nutritional analysis per serving:

Cake:

257	Calories	45 %	Calories from Fat
5 g	Protein	3 g	Fiber
30 g	Carbohydrates	59 mg	Sodium
13 g	Fat	0 mg	Cholesterol

Glaze:

77	Calories	58 %	Calories from Fat
1 g	Protein	0 g	Fiber
7 g	Carbohydrates	6 mg	Sodium
5 g	Fat	0 mg	Cholesterol

Total:

334	Calories	48 %	Calories from Fat
6 g	Protein	3 g	Fiber
37 g	Carbohydrates	65 mg	Sodium
18 g	Fat	0 mg	Cholesterol

Walnut Layer Cake

This elegant cake is richly flavored with Grand Marnier, apricot preserves, and a tart white icing. It is stunning when topped with an apricot rose.

16 servings

Walnut Cake
1 cup bread flour
1/2 cup granulated sugar
1/2 tablespoon baking powder
1/4 teaspoon salt
1/2 cup chopped walnuts
1/3 cup buttermilk
1 egg
1 egg white
1/4 cup pear baby food
1 tablespoon canola oil
1 teaspoon vanilla

Grand Marnier Filling
3 tablespoons Grand Marnier
1 egg white
1/2 cup granulated sugar
1/2 tablespoon cornstarch

Apricot Glaze
1/2 cup good-quality apricot preserves

White Icing
1 egg white, at room temperature
1/2 teaspoon fresh lemon juice
1 teaspoon vanilla
2 cups powdered sugar

1 cup chopped walnuts (optional)
apricot rose (page 274, optional)

Preheat oven to 350 degrees.

To make walnut cake: Combine flour, granulated sugar, baking powder, salt, and walnuts in a large mixing bowl.

Combine buttermilk, egg, egg white, pears, oil, and vanilla in a small bowl and blend well. Add buttermilk mixture to dry ingredients and mix with a fork until blended. Spoon batter into a 9-inch round cake pan that has been coated with vegetable spray and bake for 20 minutes, or until cake tester inserted into center of cake comes out clean. Cover cake with waxed paper and cool on a cake rack for 10 minutes. Remove cake from pan, recover with waxed paper, and let cool completely.

To make Grand Marnier filling: Place Grand Marnier, egg white, granulated sugar, and cornstarch in a small heavy saucepan over moderate heat and bring to a boil, stirring constantly. Let mixture boil for 2 to 3 minutes, or until it thickens, stirring constantly. Remove saucepan from heat and bring to room temperature, or until thick enough to spread. Set aside.

To make apricot glaze: Place apricot preserves in small heavy saucepan over moderate heat; bring to a boil. Set aside.

To make white icing: Place egg white, lemon juice, vanilla and 1 cup powdered sugar in mixing bowl of electric mixer and beat with whisk attachment until blended. Add remaining sugar and beat several minutes, or until icing is thick enough to spread.

When ready to assemble cake: Split cake layer in half using a serrated knife. Place first layer on a 9-inch cardboard round or cake plate and place 3-inch strips of waxed paper under edges of cake (this will prevent icing from getting on clean plate). Spread Grand Marnier filling on top of first cake layer; top with second cake layer. Spread apricot glaze over top and sides of cake and let sit 10 minutes. After glaze has set, spread white icing over top and sides of cake. Refrigerate cake for several hours, or overnight. Bring to room temperature before serving.

Note: For a dramatic-looking cake, center a glass upside down on top of the iced cake. Press 1 cup chopped walnuts on sides and top of cake, just up to the glass. Remove glass and place an apricot rose in the center.

Nutritional analysis per serving:

Cake:

455	Calories	7 %	Calories from Fat
3 g	Protein	1 g	Fiber
104 g	Carbohydrates	192 mg	Sodium
4 g	Fat	13 mg	Cholesterol

Cake with walnut topping:

503	Calories	15 %	Calories from Fat
4 g	Protein	2 g	Fiber
105 g	Carbohydrates	193 mg	Sodium
8 g	Fat	13 mg	Cholesterol

Cake Decorations

Apricot Rose

1 rose

4 to 5 moist dried apricots

Using sharp scissors, remove and discard the slightly thickened edge around the apricots. With a rolling pin, roll out each apricot between 2 pieces of waxed paper to about a thickness of $1/16$ to $2/16$ inch. With the sticky side of an apricot facing in, roll tightly into a cone shape to form the bud of the rose. With the wide end down, wrap another flattened apricot loosely around the bud. Repeat with remaining apricots to form the rose by gently peeling back apricots. Secure the bottom of the rose with a toothpick and remove any excess. Store the apricot rose in an airtight container until ready to use. The apricot rose can be lightly brushed with melted apricot preserves to make it look glossy.

Chocolate Curls

Makes enough curls to top one cake

1 cup chocolate chips

Place chocolate chips in a small heavy saucepan, covered, over very low heat. When chocolate is soft enough to blend, stir well. Pour chocolate onto a baking sheet into a 4 × 4-inch square and smooth the top with a spatula. Let chocolate sit at room temperature for 1 hour or more until chocolate is relatively firm. With a cheese slicer that has a flat blade and a slot at the bottom of the blade, press the blade flat on the chocolate and slide it across to make curls. If the chocolate is too soft, allow it to sit for 15 to 30 minutes, testing it every now and then. You will know when it is the right consistency because this method creates beautiful curls.

Humidity and temperature are major factors in the timing. Additionally, any broken chocolate may be melted again and reset. Store chocolate curls in an airtight container in the freezer or refrigerator if not using them right away.

Dark or White Chocolate Rose

3 to 4 roses

4 ounces white or semisweet chocolate, chopped
2 tablespoons light corn syrup

Place chocolate in a small heavy saucepan, covered, over low heat. Cook just until chocolate is soft enough to blend. Add corn syrup and immediately blend mixture. Pour chocolate onto a baking sheet that has been coated with vegetable spray. Refrigerate for 30 to 40 minutes, or until almost firm.

Place chocolate on work surface and knead until it is pliable. For each rose, remove a small piece and roll it into a ball, then form it into a cone to be used as the base of the rose; set aside. Place remaining chocolate between two pieces of waxed paper and roll it out until 1/16 inch thick. Cut three 1-inch circles, three to four 1 1/4-inch circles, and three to four 1 1/2-inch circles. Or make larger or smaller cirlces, depending on the size of the rose desired. Wrap a 1-inch circle around base of reserved cone. Wrap another small circle, slightly overlapping the first one. Continue doing this with the circles, ending with the larger ones. If not using the rose immediately, it can be stored in an airtight container until ready to use.

Note: This recipe can also be used to make ribbons or bows. Roll the chocolate into 1-inch-wide strips and tie them into a bow or make them into curls.

Glazed Hazelnuts or Walnuts

15 to 20 hazelnuts or walnuts

1/4 cup sugar
2 tablespoons water

Place toothpicks in nuts and set aside.

Combine sugar and water in a small heavy saucepan; blend well. Without stirring, cook mixture, covered, over medium heat until it begins to simmer. Continue to cook for 2 to 3 minutes. Remove cover and cook until mixture turns a rich golden brown. Dip nuts into caramelized mixture until completely coated; rest toothpick on rim of a cake pan so the nuts do not touch anything. When nuts are cool, use scissors to remove any excess caramel that may have dripped while cooling. Remove and discard toothpicks.

White Chocolate Cobweb

2 ounces white chocolate, melted

This technique should be used immediately after chocolate glaze is applied to cake. Spoon white chocolate into a pastry bag fitted with a small writing tip. Pipe a circle around the top edge of cake; then another circle about 1 inch in from the first. Continue this procedure until the cake is covered with concentric circles. Immediately take the tip of a knife or toothpick and draw a line from center of the cake to the edge. Draw another line from the edge, 1 inch from the first line, and bring it to the center. Continue around cake, alternately running knife from center to edge, then edge to center of cake until you have created a cobweb.

Index

Pineapple filling, 204–206
Pineapple frosting, 204–206
Pineapple Muffins, 152–153
Pineapple Tea Bread, 45–46
Poppy seed almond bread, 2–3
Poppy Seed and Cinnamon Cake, 47–48
Poppy Seed Muffins, 154–155
Pound cake, Southwestern, 55–56
Prune Gourmet, The, 89
Prune-pecan bread, lowfat, 37–38
Prune purée, 98
Pudding
    apple, 167–168
    citrus bread, 174–175
    lemon mousse, 191–192
    peach, 202–203
    pumpkin flan, 211–212
    whiskey bread, 228–229
Pumpkin bars, trick-or-treat, 117–118
Pumpkin bread
    cranberry, 24–25
    muffins, 156–157
    raisin and walnut, 49–50
    spiced, 57–58
Pumpkin Cheesecake, 208–210
Pumpkin cookies, harvest-time, 87–88
Pumpkin cupcakes, sugar-and-spice, 223–224
Pumpkin Flan, 211–212
Pumpkin-Gingerbread Cake, 213–215
Pumpkin Muffins, 156–157
Pumpkin, Raisin, and Walnut Bread, 49–50
Purée
    cantaloupe, 218–219
    prune, 98

R

Raisin and chocolate chip cookies, 68
Raisin bars, banana, 66–67
Raisin bran muffins, refrigerator, 160–161

Raisin coffee cake, Italian, 34–35
Raisin, oatmeal, and millet cookies, 100–101
Raisin, pumpkin, and walnut bread, 49–50
Raisins and pumpkin cookies, 87–88
Raspberry Muffins, 158–159
Raspberry sauce, 253–255
Refrigerator cookies, chocolate-nut, 72–73
Refrigerator Raisin Bran Muffins, 160–161
Regal Chocolate Torte, 259–261
Rhubarb Cake Squares, 51–52
Rose decorations
    apricot, 274
    chocolate, dark or white, 275
Rosette decorations, 184, 187, 206, 232
Rosh Hashana, 32
Rum-Apple Cake, 216–217
Rum sauce, 216–217

S

Sacher, Eduard, 262
Sachertorte, 262–264
Salted Peanut and Chocolate Chip Cookies, 108–109
Sauces
    citrus, 174
    raspberry, 253–255
    rum, 216–217
    strawberry, 178–179
    whiskey, 228–229
Sensational Chocolate Torte, 265–267
Seven-minute frosting, 244–245
Solo Lowfat Brownies, 110–111
Sorbet, strawberry and kiwi, 218–219
Sour cream
    blueberry coffee cake, 11–12
    coffee cake, 53–54
Sour Cream Coffee Cake, 53–54
Southwestern Pound Cake, 55–56